With fresh insights into familiar Bible passages and in opening her heart and life to readers, author Donna Pyle has tackled the topic of forgiveness. Readers will want to grab a journal to document the lessons and Bible verses the author encourages readers to write down, helping to imprint God's truths. Thank you, Donna, for delving into an area where many people struggle. Thank you even more for leading readers to God's Word for the answers.

—*Janice Wendorf,*
past LWML president

In *Forgiveness*, Donna tackles the universal struggles that underlie extending and receiving grace in our fallen world. She identifies and corrects common misbeliefs about forgiveness, defines biblical restitution, and discusses key biblical examples of forgiveness. Donna addresses revenge, bitterness, and all the ways we can respond to our wounds in the flesh, yet uses Scripture and beautiful language to remind us of the power of Jesus at work in us, making forgiveness in every relationship possible. *Forgiveness* is the perfect comprehensive approach for studying a topic that affects us all.

—*Angie Goeke, author of* A Girl and Her Warhorse,
musician, and speaker

With her trademark warm, candid style, Bible teacher and author Donna Pyle invites you into the life-transforming journey of true forgiveness. Turn these pages, immerse yourself in God's comforting, refining Word, and walk with Donna away from the burden of bitterness and into the liberating lightness of forgiveness.

—*Michelle DeRusha, author of* Katharina and Martin Luther:
The Radical Marriage of a Runaway Nun and a Renegade Monk

Donna Pyle's latest book on forgiveness is a welcome new resource for individuals or groups to discover more on both the process and intricacies of something that is meant to shape so much of our daily walk of faith: forgiving one another in love and truth. Donna covers the depth and the breadth of damage that unforgiveness can reap in our hearts and lives, but shines light on the freedom we are given in Jesus Christ. She recognizes the losses involved in forgiveness, and she doesn't shy away from calling out the lies and cultural myths that stand as barriers to forgiveness and freedom. She covers a wide range of experiences and offenses when forgiveness can enter in and offer much needed restoration, including adultery, abuse, family turmoil, habitual sins, to name only a few. The book is in a helpful format utilizing beautiful language, questions that root around Scripture and our personal experiences, and optional small-group sections. *Forgiveness* offers an authentic look at the pain of life's journey, but reminds us on every page that we have a Savior who came to heal and renew.

—Deaconess Heidi Goehmann, writer, blogger, and speaker at I Love My Shepherd Ministries

A Small-Group Bible Study

Forgiveness

RECEIVED FROM GOD ♥ EXTENDED TO OTHERS

DONNA PYLE

CONCORDIA PUBLISHING HOUSE • SAINT LOUIS

Published 2017 by Concordia Publishing House
3558 S. Jefferson Avenue, St. Louis, MO 63118–3968
1-800-325-3040 · cph.org

2 3 4 5 6 7 8 9 10   26 25 24 23 22 21 20 19 18

Dedication

To *Jesus*

Thank You for letting
Your Word speak
Your water pour
Your bread feed
Your light shine
Your vine grow
Your love remain
Your hope endure
and Your forgiveness flow.
All for us.
In spite of the astronomical cost.
There is *none* like You.

Table of Contents

INTRODUCTION

And the Lord said, If ye had faith as a grain of mustard seed,
*ye might say unto **this sycamine** tree, Be thou plucked up by*
the root, and be thou planted in the sea; and it should obey
you. (Luke 17:6 KJV, emphasis added)

The sycamine tree was known to have one of the deepest root structures of all trees in the Middle East. A hearty and robust tree that grew to a height of thirty feet or more, its roots plunged deep into the earth, tapping into underground water sources. Blistering weather and drought posed little threat. Even shearing off the tree at its base would not guarantee its death. Because of its deep roots, it resurfaced time and again.

This tree was *incredibly* difficult to eradicate once established.

So why should we care about this tree, and what does it have to do with forgiveness? Jesus specifically used the sycamine tree to teach His disciples about unforgiveness and bitterness (see verse above). Since you are reading this book, it is safe to assume that you have struggled with one or both.

You understand how *incredibly* difficult it is to eradicate both bitterness and unforgiveness once they are established in your life.

Notice how Jesus said "*this* sycamine tree." Why not a palm tree or olive tree? The fact that Jesus used the word *this* indicates He was making specific parallels between that tree and the detrimental effects of bitterness and unforgiveness in a person's life.

The roots of bitterness and unforgiveness can grow deep into the human soul, watered by any offense that lies hidden in the soil of the heart. The offense does not stay hidden for long though. Left alone, it will establish deep roots and produce bitter fruit. Such fruit becomes evident through angry thoughts, words, and deeds.

But the sycamine tree was known for more than deep roots. The spiritual parallels between unforgiveness and the properties of the sycamine tree are chilling.

The wood from the sycamine tree was the preferred material for building coffins and caskets. The tree grew quickly in nearly any environment, making it readily available in many different places. In fact, Egyptian archaeologists today often discover little square boxes made from sycamine that contain various figurines placed at the feet of mummies. These sycamine boxes remained uncorrupted for at least three thousand years. *Three thousand years!*

Unforgiveness and bitterness build caskets around our hearts. When left unchecked, they have the power to eventually destroy every good thing in our lives: love, freedom, relationships, and transparent communion with the Father. When we bury hurt away from God's healing power, our self-made coffin can last a *very* long time.

Another startling fact about the sycamine tree? It was pollinated only by wasps. The pollination process was initiated when a wasp stuck its stinger right into the heart of the fruit. In other words, the sycamine tree's fruit had to be "stung" in order to reproduce.

Now think how many times you have heard a person say, "I've been stung by that person once, but I'm not going to be stung like that again!" Those people have been "stung" by hurt, and you can almost see the poison creeping deep into the soil of their hearts to pollinate every bitter word they utter. Stung people build coffins around their hearts to prevent being stung again. Can you hear the pounding of the casket maker's hammers?

Significantly, the sycamine tree was usually planted where two paths met. Since it had a large trunk with stout branches offering shade, travelers often paused under this tree to deliberate which path to take.

When you and I get hurt—emotionally, mentally, or spiritually—we stand at a crossroads. We have a choice between the dark, burdensome path of unforgiveness or the Son-drenched, freeing path of forgiveness.

This choice really *is* ours.

As children of the living God, we must believe that the process of eradicating bitter roots is never a hopeless endeavor. Jesus told His disciples in Luke 17:6 that uprooting unforgiveness is possible if a person has the faith of a *grain of mustard seed*. Since the gift of faith comes from God

(Ephesians 2:8), we have access to an abundant, unlimited supply of poison's antidote.

In God's hands, the casket maker's career is short lived.

Jesus taught that believers need faith to deal with unforgiveness. The good news is that if forgiveness is truly the desire of the heart, any person, through the power of the Holy Spirit, with even the tiniest measure of faith can command those roots of bitterness to shrivel up.

Faith is a container whose power lies not in being the container, but in what it contains: unsurpassing confidence in God's promises. Faith enables believers to put God's promises into practice.

The goal of this study is to dig into Scripture to gain knowledge and a clear understanding of forgiveness in order to equip ourselves with the tools to apply them to our daily walks.

This study is aimed at opening our hearts and minds to the life-altering, rich teachings that God's Word offers about forgiveness, the harm of harboring unforgiveness, and how to extend forgiveness to others. This path is infinitely difficult to walk alone, so we will underscore the value of regularly gathering with other believers in church and small groups to acknowledge and confess our sins, hear Christ's Gospel proclaimed, and receive the precious gift of forgiveness.

God the Father is the ultimate expert on forgiveness. He sent Jesus to rescue humanity, even knowing we would reject, despise, and kill Him.

Yet He sent His *only* Son *anyway*.

Through His nail-pierced sacrifice, Jesus eradicated the sting of sin and unforgiveness and removed them "as far as the east is from the west" (Psalm 103:12).

Our Lord and Savior's entire ministry on earth centered on forgiveness and love. That's why He came. He alone experienced the exorbitant price tag of forgiving all sin of all time. His sacrifice purchased the priceless gift of eternal life for everyone who believes.

Several months before writing this study, I asked on social media what people struggle with regarding forgiveness: "If you were diving into an in-depth Bible study about forgiveness, what scenarios would you deem important to cover?"

The answers were real and unvarnished. Friends, family, acquaintances, and friends of friends wrote of their struggles with forgiving intentional abuse, betrayal, family hurts, of knowing the difference between forgiveness and reconciliation, knowing how to forgive yourself (which is a myth we will set straight in this study), and knowing how to teach forgiveness. We will address all of those scenarios and more in the coming pages.

We will also learn what forgiveness is *not*. It is not forgetting, excusing a sin or crime, or approving bad behavior.

But the hardest truth we will learn is that forgiveness is *not optional*—regardless of the severity of the wound. God's command to forgive is not intended to increase our burden, but to free us from its weight. We cannot lug the millstone of unforgiveness without becoming exhausted under its load.

Jesus took our millstones of hurt and promises: *"Come to Me, all who labor and are heavy laden, and I will give you rest. Take My yoke upon you, and learn from Me, for I am gentle and lowly in heart, and you will find rest for your souls. For My yoke is easy, and My burden is light"* (Matthew 11:28–30).

I have not experienced every hurt that you have—but Jesus has. Through His life and sacrifice, we lean into this study to soak in His teaching, seek to understand His words, and move forward to embrace the freedom of forgiveness.

Because that's what true forgiveness feels like.

Freedom.

Your freedom.

How to Use This Bible Study

This small-group Bible study is designed to lead you on a path toward a more intimate relationship with God by bringing you together with fellow believers. Serious Christ followers desire to grow in their faith, obey God, and serve as valuable contributors in their families, churches, and communities.

You can walk through this study in a variety of ways: individually, in a small group, during family discussions, and in Sunday Bible classes. But may I challenge you beyond your comfort zone? Consider stepping out and asking some friends to join you in this study. Encourage your church's small group to walk through this together. Ask your pastor to offer it as a Sunday morning Bible class.

Unforgiveness and holding grudges are pandemic in our culture. One of the marks of a Christian is forgiveness. The more we gather in community to learn forgiveness and live it out daily, the more influence we as Christ followers will have on the fabric of society.

Each lesson provides valuable tools for exploring important aspects of your faith walk with other believers who also desire spiritual growth. During this process, you will get to know one another, your stories, struggles, and victories. Some will be similar, while some will differ greatly from your own, but my hope is that they will provide you with a fresh perspective.

If you are walking through this study individually, take your time. Walk through each lesson carefully, allowing time for God to move you through at your own pace. But keep moving!

Each day's individual lesson contains important times of quiet reflection and personal application to provide intimate time with the Lord between your study group's regular gatherings. It is important that you do not neglect this valuable time of being still before the Lord. It is hard to hear the still, small voice of God through His Word and prayer beyond the cacophony of the world. We love wearing the badge of busyness and often fail to take time to listen.

Each lesson concludes with time with your small group to dig into Scripture together and have meaningful discussion to discover God's truth and life application for that lesson's topic. As you and your group exchange insights, pray for God to expand your understanding of Scripture and deepen the bonds of faith, friendship, and Christ-centered purpose in your group.

One person should be designated as the group facilitator. He or she does not need to have prior training in leading a Bible study or discussion group. The facilitator will just make sure the discussion stays on track.

The facilitator can also speed up or slow down the group time by choosing to skip some discussion questions or concentrate longer on others to fit your allotted study time, ensuring that no one gets left out of the faith-building, friendship-solidifying process.

Each small group's dynamics and study pace will vary. You may complete an entire lesson each time you meet. Others may take their time to get as far in a lesson as time allows and then pick up where they left off during their next gathering. This study may take you eight weeks or eight months, but the most important focus is learning and growing in faith together.

And let's be honest, the learning and application of forgiveness is a lifelong process.

Now that your plan is in place, you are ready to embark on the journey! I pray that through this study, God transforms you more and more into the likeness of His Son.

FORGIVENESS IS ALWAYS PERSONAL

Put on then, as God's chosen ones, holy and beloved,
compassionate hearts, kindness, humility, meekness, and
patience, bearing with one another and, if one has a complaint
against another, forgiving each other; as the Lord has forgiven
you, so you also must forgive. (Colossians 3:12–13)

The bell opening my title fight against unforgiveness clanged on December 1, 2009.

DING! I discovered my husband was leading a secret, double life.

DING! He just wanted to save face, cut losses, and disappear.

DING! Nineteen years invested in that relationship down the drain.

Divorce proceedings followed. Dividing stuff that didn't matter ensued. Four fleeting months later, I had an ex-husband. Ex-dreams. An ex-me.

KNOCKOUT.

One day when everything seemed to be closing in at once, I bellowed to an empty bedroom, "I WAS FAITHFUL! MY 'YES' MEANT YES! THIS IS SO *UNFAIR!*"

Enter anger, stage left. Bitterness slithered in behind it. The orchestra wailed a mournful waltz. The audience trickled out. Stage lights faded to black.

Winter settled in.

Thankfully, that winter season didn't last long. Out of sheer exhaustion, I finally crumpled before the Lord, handing up my pain to God by the truckload during counseling.

The sun peeked out.

The thaw slowly started.

Spring flowers of hope began sprouting in my heart.

I learned a vital lesson during that time: *Forgiveness is always personal.* We cannot forgive a faceless entity. I could not feel "mad at life" and expect God to heal my heart.

When you and I feel a personal sense of being wronged or hurt, we need to be able to name a person, action, and pain in order to walk toward forgiveness. Workers who are mad at "the company" face the same struggle. Citizens who are angry at "the government" generally find themselves in the same drifting boat. No face to forgive, only anger to seethe.

Specificity is the first step toward freedom.

We struggle to extend forgiveness because our human nature does not *want* to forgive those who wound us. I certainly struggled to forgive my ex-husband. The wounds caused by his betrayals went deep.

Unforgiveness drags joy behind the shed and beats it senseless.

Pain reminds us that we are not metallic machines but frail flesh, capable of hurting and being hurt. Pain is the price of living in this broken world, being broken by it and broken in it.

But God wrote the victory chapter in our lives during six hours one Friday. At Calvary, Jesus broke once for all, the only breaking where true healing begins.

Forgiveness transforms souls shouting curses into shofars trumpeting God's praises.

Christ-centered forgiveness acknowledges our perpetrators as broken people operating through their own broken understanding of the world. It also acknowledges our own need to confess and repent. Time does not heal all wounds; God does. Thankfully, He never tires of offering us hope and a future centered in Him.

During times when I struggled to forgive those who hurt me, I prayed jagged words through the pain, hunted healing in the Word, and emptied toxic unforgiveness into tear-stained journals. I learned every Scripture passage about forgiveness and how God enables us to extend it. God used those processes to teach me how to keep very short accounts of hurt in the future.

My piles of research notes, journal entries, and Scripture passages about forgiveness could fill a book. Hence this study. God used what I learned about forgiveness during that time to teach me to apply it to every area of my life: family, church, friendships, social media trolls, unkind strangers, difficult children, and challenging co-workers.

My prayer is that through this study, He will do the same for you.

We are reminded of forgiveness every time we say the Lord's prayer: *"and forgive us our debts, as we also have forgiven our debtors"* (Matthew 6:12).

It is a simple prayer, yet hard.

Forgiveness means sharing the unmitigated grace we have already received; it is the extension of hope so others might discover the Source of all hope.

Unless we live in isolation, each of us regularly experiences times when we are wronged. It starts when our expectations are not met, when a complete stranger makes a simple mistake, or when a loved one commits a willful act. We feel the stings of disappointment, anger, and bitterness. Deep wounds take a long time to heal, and if we hold on to that hurt for a long time, our hearts become hardened.

A vital part of this study includes unpacking some harmful myths that many of us believe about forgiveness. One of the most harmful myths is that holding on to unforgiveness means we retain some kind of power or control over our offender. Nothing could be further from the truth. Withholding forgiveness is a self-made jail cell. Christ died to liberate us. Unforgiveness stagnates our relationship with God in sinful disobedience. I have learned those two truths firsthand thanks to wise pastors and counselors.

Learning to forgive is a difficult task. Been there. Done that. Have five T-shirts. It requires humility, maturity, and grace, which we receive from God. Forgiveness means that we confess our own part in the situation—such as harboring unforgiveness!—and repent so we can release our wounded pride, anger, and revenge to God and receive His gracious love.

The truth is that no one's transgression against you or wound you have sustained exceeds your transgressions against God. Yet He has completely forgiven you.

Because God set the example in Christ, He commands us to forgive from the heart all of our trespassers. Perhaps we recite the Lord's Prayer so often in church that we no longer hear or heed its message: "and forgive us our debts, as we also have forgiven our debtors" (Matthew 6:12). We confess our sins and ask God to forgive our debts (or trespasses)—but stop short before obeying the second half of that prayer.

You and I cannot forgive in our own power. "To err is human, to forgive divine" is true. And we are not divine. But God's divine power residing in the heart of every believer enables us to extend forgiveness without reservation. It is not possible to hold love and hate in the same heart. I've tried it. It doesn't work.

Forgiveness is a humanizing, dignifying, redemptive act of God.

Forgiveness frees us from the narrative of hate.

Forgiveness liberates us from our prisons.

Forgiveness equals abundant life.

Forgiveness moves us toward others to extend the Gospel of grace.

That is why forgiveness is not optional.

I pray that God accomplishes much for you during this study.

DAY 1:
UNDERSTANDING
FORGIVENESS

As far as the east is from the west, so far does He remove our transgressions from us. (Psalm 103:12)

If you asked a dozen people to define forgiveness, you would likely hear twelve different responses. Since Christians are commanded to extend forgiveness, we need to clearly understand what it means.

Webster's dictionary defines *forgive* as "to excuse a fault or offense; to stop feeling anger or resentment against; and to absolve from payment of." *Excuse* and *absolve* are difficult verbs to swallow in the context of pain.

The New Testament word *forgive* in Greek is *aphiēmi*, which means "to send away." In Christ, God packed up our transgressions and permanently sent them away. According to Psalm 103:12, how far did He send them?

_____

_____

The thing about east and west is that there is *no end*. Once you start heading east, you are always heading east until you change directions. Once you journey west, you are always journeying west.

When someone hurts us, God commands us to forgive because hate and bitterness do not line up with His teaching to love. Thankfully, He does not simply issue the command, sit back, and watch us struggle. He provides the Source of power that enables us to fulfill His command.

Write out Galatians 2:20.

_____

_____

Hate and love cannot coexist. Forgiveness cannot blossom when roots of unforgiveness hide in the soil of our hearts.

Jesus talked about forgiveness more than two dozen times in the Gospels, including a key part of the Lord's Prayer (Matthew 6:12) and teaching His disciples to forgive others "seventy-seven times" (Matthew 18:22). He even asked God to forgive those who nailed Him to the cross (Luke 23:34). That includes you and me.

Forgiveness is not God's suggestion; it is His command. Write out Colossians 3:12–13.

_____

_____

Did you notice the little word *must?* We *must* also forgive. That's a hard truth to digest when the mere thought of forgiving someone makes you sick to your stomach.

It's amazing how easily we throw around the word *forgiveness* until we are asked to step forward through the pain and extend it personally. But forgiveness is the only way we will survive bleeding out from the spiritual and emotional wounds caused by the hurtful words and actions of others.

The heart of forgiveness always beats with liberation and freedom. Not necessarily for those who hurt you. But *for you*.

Forgiveness is costly. We struggle not to lash out at those who hurt us. We're absorbing the debt and cost of the consequences instead of taking it out on the perpetrator.

We suffer, and it hurts terribly. Some say it feels like dying. They are not wrong. The cost of forgiveness is death.

Just ask Jesus.

Yet it is a death that leads to resurrection.

So start by asking God for just one small step *today* on the road toward forgiveness. Tomorrow, ask Him for another small step.

The road ends in the death of bitterness and a resurrection to life.

The dead-end road ends at Calvary.

Pause
for Quiet Reflection

Intentionally schedule at least fifteen minutes of quiet time before the Lord with pen and paper in hand. Ask Him to still your busy mind and open your heart. Take your time reflecting on these questions, and then write down your answers.

1. **Identify a hurt that you have not yet forgiven. Why are you holding on to it?**

_____

_____

2. **How has holding on to that unforgiveness affected your life? those around you?**

_____

_____

Apply
It Personally

Now that this lesson has provided some insight from the Word about the basics of forgiveness, review what you wrote in the Quiet Reflection section above.

Forgiveness is a battle that no one can fight for you. It requires intentionality and prayer. So, let's get specific right now. Attach a name and face to your hurt. If you have trouble putting a face to your hurt, start there by asking God to provide one. When you can see them clearly (not a faceless entity), pray specifically for God to soften your heart against that person or persons. Each time you approach the Lord's Table, lay your hurt at His feet and receive Jesus' forgiveness. Relentlessly, ask Him to work forgiveness in you and then through you.

You might pray through gritted teeth like I used to. It's okay. God still listens and will begin to faithfully grant your desire.

God has you in the palm of His hand as you walk through this study individually and together as a group. He promises to bring beauty from ashes, so keep walking.

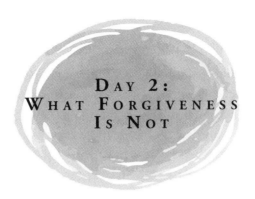

DAY 2:
WHAT FORGIVENESS
IS NOT

*If we confess our sins, [God] is faithful and just to forgive us
our sins and to cleanse us from all unrighteousness.* (1 John 1:9)

The hardest struggle I faced in forgiving those who hurt me was believing that if I extended forgiveness to them, I was somehow condoning their actions.

That lie comes straight from the devil.

The enemy loves weaving a web of toxicity around that lie because we want those who hurt us to pay for their transgressions. Although I didn't want blood to compensate for my pain, there certainly was a part of me that wanted to see my offenders hurting as much as I was.

But therein lies the problem. Sometimes we never again see those who hurt us, so if we tie forgiveness to that condition, we embrace misplaced rage and a hardened heart.

Sometimes we struggle to forgive our trespassers because it feels like we are stamping "APPROVED" on their sinful acts. But forgiveness does not mean condoning someone's behavior. Those are separate issues that we will address below.

As God faithfully opens doors for me to travel and speak with groups of women all over the country, I have discovered that forgiveness is often misunderstood.

Some believe that forgiveness can only be granted when their perpetrator asks for it. Others believe that forgiveness means you must reconcile with the person who hurt you and live in joy-filled harmony. Neither could be further from the truth.

In order to extend forgiveness, we need to clearly understand what it is *not*.

Forgiveness Is Not Excusing a Sin or Crime.

This is one of the most common objections to extending forgiveness. Many people often equate forgiveness with letting someone off the hook; like somehow forgiveness approves what they did because we didn't force them to make it right. But that's not what forgiveness means.

For instance, a rape victim suffers horrible atrocities, and there are legal consequences for the violator. The victim can forgive her attacker yet still follow the legal process to take the proper course for her attacker to reap the punishment for his actions. Sin is not okay. It can be forgiven, but it should not be excused. By God's grace, we become wiser regarding future interactions with that person.

Forgiveness Is Different from Reconciliation.

Forgiveness is extended by one individual to another. Reconciliation takes two people who agree to set aside past hurtful behavior, communicate to repair the relationship, and move forward together.

I realized that reconciliation for my marriage was not possible due to the kind of women with whom my ex-husband was involved. If we had reconciled and continued in our marriage, I stood a very real chance of contracting HPV, HIV or AIDS. My ex-husband was a habitual adulterer, even when given additional chances, so reconciling and remaining married would have placed my health (and ultimately my life) in danger.

In situations where habitual abuse (whether physical or verbal) has occurred, reconciliation may not be possible because behaviors may not change and safe boundaries must be established. But forgiveness is still commanded. We will dive deeper into this issue in Lesson 3.

Forgiveness Is Not about Justice or Consequences.

Forgiveness does not obligate the forgiver to protect the offender from reaping the consequences of his or her actions. Consequences are usually what it takes for offenders to change their behavior. If their actions have broken the law (rape, harming a child, etc.), we can and should follow through with appropriate legal action. To prevent a perpetrator from raping again, testifying at trial is certainly appropriate. There are always consequences for sin, but exacting those consequences is God's job, not ours. Even in such awful circumstances when reconciliation is not possible, we still move toward forgiveness.

Forgiveness Is Not about the Offender.

It is not our job to determine whether someone deserves forgiveness. God never tells us in His Word to extend it only when the offender begs for it. Some people hold grudges and stay angry until they believe their offender has suffered enough. But how do we determine when enough is enough?

Hate and anger have consuming power, and those toxins can control and define us. When we allow unforgiveness to consume us, the object of our wrath actually has control over us. It can keep our heart dangling over the fire, so to speak. We are washed clean by baptismal grace; therefore, God does not withhold forgiveness from us—and we are to follow His lead.

Offering forgiveness to our offender is primarily obedience to God's command. Yet it is also a gift to ourselves of a life free from bitterness and anger.

Write out Colossians 3:23–25.

_____

_____

Did you notice that the Lord is the focus of those verses? The Lord handles the wrongs done to us as we heartily serve Him.

Forgiveness Is Not Artificial Nonchalance.

Have you ever tried to pretend someone's actions or words did not hurt you? Me too. But when I remember that hurt for the tenth time in an hour, I cannot keep pretending.

Pretending there is nothing to forgive results in anger and resentment down the road. What we harbor internally eventually surfaces externally. Forgiveness means we acknowledge the hurtful actions or words, pray for God to provide insight on how best to convey them gracefully to the offender, and allow God to move us toward Him for healing.

Forgiveness Is Not Avoidance.

Some people believe that out of sight means out of mind. As long as we avoid our offender, everything will be just fine. Although that person may not be around, the hurt they inflicted remains. It must be acknowledged, grieved, and forgiven.

Forgiveness Is Not Easy.

It's just not. It takes time. If the wound is deep, it may take a long time. But focusing our energy and time on moving toward forgiveness means embracing our future free from the bondage of vengeful toxins.

We can confidently count on God's outrageous faithfulness to us. Yesterday is over. Your future lies ahead. Relentlessly lay those hurts at His feet and trust Him to remove the sting.

Forgiveness is not "giving in."

Forgiveness is an act of liberation and new life.

For you.

Pause
for Quiet Reflection

Intentionally schedule at least fifteen minutes of quiet time before the Lord with pen and paper in hand. Ask Him to still your busy mind and open your heart. Take your time reflecting on these questions, and then write down your answers.

1. **As you read through the truths about what forgiveness is *not*, did any resonate personally with you? Which ones? Please explain.**

_____

_____

2. If the tables were reversed and you were the offender, how would your perspective of offering forgiveness more readily change?

_____

_____

Apply
It Personally

Now that this lesson has provided some insight from the Word about what forgiveness is not, review what you wrote in the Quiet Reflection section above. In light of the one area that you struggle in the most, take time right now to go before the Lord in repentant prayer and ask Him to give you the insight, strength, and willingness to move through it with His help.

God has you in the palm of His hand as you walk through this study individually and together as a group. He promises to bring beauty from ashes, so keep walking.

Behold, I will bring to it health and healing, and I will heal
them and reveal to them abundance of prosperity and security.

(Jeremiah 33:6)

I forgive you," says a father to the gunman who murdered his child in a drive-by shooting. When the father wakes up tomorrow, he will forgive him again and again and again.

"I forgive you," says an elderly woman to the criminal who cleaned out her life's savings. When she remembers it once more, she will forgive her again.

"I forgive you," says a brother to the drunk driver who maimed his sister. Each time he sees his sister, he will forgive the driver again.

The truth about forgiveness is that it is not a one-step, one-stop process. The deeper the hurt, the longer the process. Yet God specifically uses forgiveness to transform us into the likeness of His Son. Jesus forgave. He set the example that we are commanded to follow.

In our human nature, when someone hurts us deeply, feelings toward forgiveness seem counterintuitive. When the initial sting of hurt subsides, anger and self-righteous indignation invade. The enemy launches debilitating ambushes, effectively turning our minds into deadly battlefields.

Self-directed, self-justifying conversations often happen when someone hurts us deeply: *"Who does he think he is treating me like that?" "If lying gave out degrees, he'd have a PhD." "I hope God hurls lightning bolts at him until he's crispy fried."* Not pretty, but real.

It is difficult for others to see the war zone, because the battles rage in our hearts and minds. However, they can certainly feel the ravages and see the effects of our internal battlefields if they venture too close to pain central. Harsh words. Withdrawal. Aggression.

As I scoured Scripture for key verses about forgiveness, God brought one in particular to the top of the stack.

Write out Colossians 3:12–13.

_____

_____

My heart and mind were often far removed from any of those godly attributes when I struggled to forgive.

You may be in a similar boat right now. Your hurt may be too fresh to move toward forgiveness today. That's okay. It takes time to process pain. But engage in the process and allow God to do a mighty work in and through you. Take courage in knowing that God has already forgiven you all of your sins; He released you of those sins in your Baptism. And He will continue to give you the strength to forgive your offender, as well. As His children with His Spirit residing in us, we operate in _His_ strength, not ours.

The bottom line is that the heart knows no time. It is unrealistic to say, "Okay, you've been mourning for four months. You should have moved on by now." Be patient. If you truly desire to forgive those who hurt you, God promises to give you the desires of your heart. In _His_ timing.

What does Psalm 37:4 tell us?

_____

_____

Forgiveness is always a process because our memory is long when it comes to hurt. If you were abused as a child, it may take years or even decades of forgiving those hurts one by one, brick by brick, in order to dismantle the wall of unforgiveness.

The road toward forgiveness travels straight through the grieving process. In grief, we cast our burdens on Him—and keep casting without snatching them back to process alone. We delve into the truth of the Word, which persistently reminds us of His love, and ultimately we experience hope.

What does Hebrews 6:19–20 tell us?

_____

_____

God alone is our sure and steadfast anchor! His hope slips behind the facades we erect to bring healing found only through Him.

Professionals generally agree that there are five main stages of grief, though some list as many as twelve. I discovered that some grief stages can linger longer than others. Sometimes, I dealt with several stages at once depending on the circumstances. You may find that true as well.

Grief Stage 1: Denial

The first reaction to being hurt is to deny the reality of the situation. This is especially true if the hurt comes from those we love and trust. Rationalizing overwhelming emotions serves as a defense mechanism to buffer shock. We may block out words or actions that hide ugly truths. This temporary shock and numbness carries us through the first wave of pain.

Grief Stage 2: Anger

Anger usually occurs when we feel helpless or powerless. To cope with the intense emotions, we sometimes redirect the hurt and pain into anger. Some people are "hurlers," and some are "hiders." Hurlers loudly verbalize their anger by shouting from the rooftop who hurt us and how. Hiders grieve internally, processing grief with only a few close confidants.

I have discovered that I am generally a hider. Identifying which one you are helps pinpoint when anger has entered the scene. For instance, when I have been engaged in a lively conversation and suddenly become withdrawn, it helps me realize that somewhere in the exchange a hurt has slipped under my skin. Recognizing a hurt before it turns into anger offers the space needed to lay it before the Lord for Him to heal before additional damage takes place through angry responses.

Our anger may be directed toward the one who inflicted the wound, strangers, friends, family, or even the mirror. Dealing with anger is crucial because it can exhaust us past the point of dealing with the hurt in a healthier way. We may be tempted just to give up, but giving up means living with anger seething just under the surface that can erupt at any time. God never taught us to give up; He taught us to surrender our anger to Him. How do you see that truth in the following passage?

James 1:19–20

_____

_____

Those verses do not say "don't get angry." They simply remind us to be slow to anger. Anger is not a sin, but we can sin in how we respond while we are angry.

Grief Stage 3: Bargaining

Bargaining works to counteract our feelings of helplessness and vulnerability by regaining control (either real or imagined) of our situation. Bargaining often pairs with denial as we look for any possible way to deflect the hurt.

When you start making *"If . . . then"* statements, you have reached the bargaining stage. "If she would only apologize, then everything would be all right." This stage may also include bargaining with God: "If You make them suffer for what they did, then I can put it behind me." But bargaining your way around facing the facts will only interfere with your healing process.

Grief Stage 4: Depression

When we realize the extent of what an offender's hurt has cost us, this stage of grief can debilitate us. Depression has many different faces, including exhaustion, withdrawal from family and friends, and bursting into tears without warning. Signs that you have reached this stage include trouble sleeping, loss of appetite, lack of energy and concentration, and crying spells.

Depression can spawn feelings of loneliness, emptiness, and isolation, so it is vital to deal with this stage seriously. You may need counseling, medication, or both. Do not be afraid to seek appropriate help from the Lord and trusted professionals.

Grief Stage 5: Acceptance

At this final stage, we are able wholeheartedly to extend forgiveness with a sense of peace from the Lord. Unfortunately, some do not reach this stage.

Acceptance does not always involve a celebration with flowers; there is usually a lingering sadness marked by calm and withdrawal. For me, calm and withdrawal look like long, uninterrupted walks listening to worship music. It provides time to ponder my situation and how God has worked it in. The more I walk, the more God moves me toward happiness and laughter once again. Acceptance lets go of the hurt, releases the offender, and allows you to move forward into new life.

The apostle Paul reminds us that even though we grieve through the forgiveness process, we do not grieve as those who have no hope.

Write out 1 Thessalonians 4:13.

_____

_____

The Lord is our hope. Forgiveness is like a diamond in the rough. Each time we extend forgiveness, God chisels away hard outer layers of hurt, rejection, confusion, ego, and narcissism to reveal God's beauty within us.

The need both to extend and receive forgiveness and mercy echoes throughout every beating heart. Peeling back those damaged, bruised layers frees our hearts to beat at maximum love for God and others.

With the same power that God used in raising Christ from the dead, He reaches down in love to offer His healing salve and rescue you from debilitating pain. He never, ever leaves us alone on this battlefield.

And He is 100 percent faithful to keep His promises. Spend time writing out and receiving encouragement from God's wonderful promises in the following verses.

Isaiah 40:29–31

_____

_____

John 14:27

_____

_____

Romans 10:9

_____

_____

Philippians 4:19

_____

_____

God gives us power and peace and also supplies everything we need to confidently walk toward forgiveness, trusting Him to accomplish it in our heart, soul, and mind.

Pause
for Quiet Reflection

Intentionally schedule at least fifteen minutes of quiet time before the Lord with pen and paper in hand. Ask Him to still your busy mind and open your heart. Take your time reflecting on these questions, and then write down your answers.

1. **As you read through the five stages of grief, which one(s) are you struggling with the most right now? Why?**

_____

_____

2. Our Savior promises: "He has sent Me to bind up the brokenhearted, to proclaim liberty to the captives . . . to comfort all who mourn; . . . to give them a beautiful headdress instead of ashes, the oil of gladness instead of mourning, the garment of praise instead of a faint spirit" (Isaiah 61:1–3). Read those verses again. What hope and comfort do they bring to you in your current grief stage?

Apply
It Personally

Now that this lesson has provided some insight from the Word that forgiveness can be a long process, review what you wrote in the Quiet Reflection section above. If you have been stuck in one grief stage for a long time, ask God right now for His wisdom to identify what has you stuck, and then ask Him to identify the tools to help you move through that stage successfully.

God has you in the palm of His hand as you walk through this study individually and together as a group. He promises to bring beauty from ashes, so keep walking.

DAY 4:
CAN WE REALLY
FORGIVE AND
FORGET?

I, I am He who blots out your transgressions for My own sake,
and I will not remember your sins. (Isaiah 43:25)

When my ex-husband committed his first adultery six years into our marriage, I did not tell anyone. I was ashamed that perhaps people would think I was a bad wife, had done something to turn him away, or the worst, I wasn't "putting out" enough.

I sought God constantly for the grace to forgive. In tears, I often knelt at His Table for forgiveness, pleading for the strength to move on. For the courage to be intimate in my marriage again. For trust in my spouse to be repaired. God granted all of those requests and more. Forgiveness flowed, our relationship was repaired, and our marriage was saved.

But I never forgot what happened.

When you are wronged, you are handed a wound. The larger the pain, the larger the wound. Just because you cannot see internal wounds does not mean you forget they exist.

We've all heard the phrase "forgive and forget." It's easy to say but impossible to do. While we may be able to forget small slights, we remember life-altering wounds.

Interestingly, remembering is usually a benefit. Our memory can instruct us on how to avoid the similar hurt in the future. For instance, I don't touch hot stoves because I did that once. Lesson learned. We remember when someone hurts us, but through God's strength we do not allow the ramifications from those hurts (such as anger, resentment, and revenge) to control our future.

The lie of *forgive and forget* makes people believe that they have the power to erase their own memories.

When we buy into the forgive-and-forget lie, we end up berating ourselves when we remember our wounds. We get frustrated and down on ourselves. We spend time and energy trying to make ourselves forget again. What a useless, unproductive cycle!

The enemy loves the forgive-and-forget lie because it wastes our time and energy and always lands us right back where we started: remembering the wound. There is no solution to the lie of forgive and forget.

Our human memories are long when it comes to remembering hurt. We do not have the power to erase our own memories. However, we can choose to keep putting our pasts behind us.

Write out what the apostle Paul said in Philippians 3:13.

_____

_____

Paul is not claiming to have the power to erase his memory. The meaning here is that he does not *care*. He acknowledges that past sins forgiven by God have no bearing on what God has planned for his future.

Yes, you and I can and should learn from past sins, but we are not required to live in their toxic brew. God has completely forgiven them through Christ's work on the cross.

When someone hands you a wound, you have three main options:

1. Hand it back. When you hand back a wound, it is called revenge. It looks something like this: "You did this to me? Then, *this* is what I will do to you." You then throw the wound back at them with a vengeance. Whether verbally or physically, handing the wound back through revenge intends harm.

2. Internalize or hide it. This happens when shame plays a part in the wound. Rape victims deal with this because some people still believe the nauseating assumption that somehow the victim invited or deserved it. The victim may hide it to avoid being called loose. Shame is the single biggest factor in hiding a wound.

3. Hand it up to Jesus. When we hand our wounds up to Jesus, we take them out of circulation. The wounds do not have the opportunity to fester in us or spread to others. Taking the wounds out of circulation stops the cycle. That is how Jesus patterned forgiveness. He felt the wounds, absorbed the pains, and forgave them from the cross. And He renews our strength to surrender our wounds to Him every time we kneel at His Table.

In Genesis 16, we see what happened when Abraham's wife, Sarah, could not conceive the children she desperately desired. She mourned, wept, and cried out to God. Instead of *"forgetting what lies behind"* as Paul later taught in Philippians 3:13, Sarah took matters into her own hands and gave her maid Hagar to Abraham so that Sarah might have children with Abraham through Hagar.

When Hagar conceived, Sarah thought that perhaps all was well. But then bitterness and jealously showed up on the scene. Even though you and I cannot "forget" a wound, we can certainly choose how to deal with it going forward.

Paul chose to leave the past in the past. Sarah did not.

Only God can truly forget a sin. Write out Hebrews 8:12.

_____

_____

God promises to forget our sins (the precise meaning of which could fill a whole book), but that is an unrealistic standard to put on ourselves. We are not God. *Thank God.*

When we link forgiving to forgetting, that misconception can lead people to think that they have never forgiven because they still remember that wound from time to time.

God's memory is infinite and unfathomable, yet He can choose to forget. What does Hebrews 10:16–18 say?

_____

_____

The phrase *"remember no more"* is a Greek double negative, which means that the combination of those words strengthen the emphatic meaning. It signifies that *"not at all"* or *"by no means"* will God remember our sins.

Forgiveness allows us to remember the good that God has brought out of our wounds, thank Him for His healing, and move forward stronger than before. God never tires of taking our burdens upon Himself. He will *never* refuse delivery.

The way of the cross means handing our pain over to Jesus instead of passing it on. Christ provides the avenue to transform our wounds from destructive impulse to creative power.

The cross is God's way of saying, *"The pain stops here."*

Thank You, Lord.

Pause
for Quiet Reflection

Intentionally schedule at least fifteen minutes of quiet time before the Lord with pen and paper in hand. Ask Him to still your busy mind and open your heart. Take your time reflecting on these questions, and then write down your answers.

1. **Out of the three ways that we usually handle wounds as noted earlier, which one describes your usual method?**

_____

_____

2. **Has someone ever given you the advice to just "forgive and forget" a wound? How did that make you want to respond?**

_____

_____

Apply
It Personally

Now that this lesson has provided some insight from the Word about the devastating lie that forgiveness equals forgetting, review what you wrote in the Quiet Reflection section above. What new truth that we discussed in this day's lesson about "forgive and forget" helps you respond differently?

_____

_____

God has you in the palm of His hand as you walk through this study individually and together as a group. He promises to bring beauty from ashes, so keep walking.

*Say to those who have an anxious heart, "Be strong; fear
not! Behold, your God will come with vengeance, with the
recompense of God. He will come and save you."* (Isaiah 35:4)

Samson had an anger problem. Or maybe he just never learned how to
process his anger well. In Judges 15, an incident between Samson and
his father-in-law eventually escalated into battles involving nations and the
slaughter of thousands of innocent people.

All because of revenge.

When Samson returned home to his wife, write out what happened in
Judges 15:1–2:

_____

_____

In a rage, how does Samson respond in Judges 15:3–5?

_____

_____

Since his father-in-law was a Philistine (Judges 14:1), Samson declared
war on the Philistines by destroying their grain fields and olive orchards
with fire (using a very animal-unfriendly method, might I add).

Such destruction affected the Philistines both economically and
religiously because they believed in gods of harvest, among other gods.

In retaliatory revenge, the Philistines burned Samson's wife and father-in-law to death (Judges 15:6).

Samson vowed not to stop his rampage until he exacted revenge for those two deaths. He subsequently attacked and slaughtered many Philistines (Judges 15:7–8).

The Philistines took their revenge up another notch by hunting down Samson, attacking the town of Lehi on the way. Then three thousand men of Judah confronted the Philistines to ask why they were coming against them. When the Philistines named Samson as the culprit, the men of Judah found Samson and handed him over to the Philistines (Judges 15:9–13).

But Samson's revenge was not finished. He picked up the jawbone of a donkey and killed one thousand men with it. *One thousand men!* All of this destruction and mayhem started with Samson, his father-in-law, and a goat.

In light of this story, there are some important truths and distinctions we need to understand about revenge. There are two basic types of revenge.

Active revenge: This kind of revenge moves aggressively toward our offenders. Perhaps a family member says something derogatory about your spouse. You immediately take offense and start telling the rest of the family about their many faults (whether secret or not). Active revenge always hurts far more people than we realize.

Passive revenge: This kind of revenge deceptively looks like forgiveness. Passive revenge does not move aggressively toward the offender, but takes the form of withholding, cold shoulders, or secretly celebrating when something negative happens to them. It is forgiveness lip service, not a genuine movement toward it.

Revenge tells God, "You're in my seat." When I choose to take revenge, I alone determine the severity of a person's transgression, the proper method of punishment, and the time frame in which it needs to occur. Revenge inflates the ego because I alone determine that God is not moving fast enough or meting out what I believe is appropriate judgment. Consequently, I take matters into my own hands and execute judgment. Revenge means failing to entrust my wound to God's justice.

Revenge always escalates. An offense can start with something as small as the rolling of eyes at someone's behavior in a social setting. But it doesn't end with reciprocated rolling eyes. It always escalates. Remember Shakespeare's Romeo and Juliet? The feud between the Capulets and the

Montagues was "bred on an airy [misspoken] word." Multiple civil brawls later, Romeo and Juliet died in their efforts to be together.

Revenge always inflames. Revenge creates an inflated ego that says, "I have the *right* to pay back the hurt they inflicted on me." And back and forth it goes.

Revenge is essentially relational ping-pong. Others can almost see it in the air. Have you ever started a new job and felt an atmosphere of "tiptoeing" around a certain person or topic? What about family reunions? There's an old story that some generation(s) ago someone did something, so now *that* part of the extended family will *never* be invited.

Forgiveness begins when you drop the jawbone.

When you find yourself in a situation where there is a nonstop back and forth, decide to put down the jawbone of revenge and back away. Forgiveness starts by refusing to participate in the game and stepping forward to end it.

The anger we feel from pain makes revenge seem logical. But anger can escalate quickly into rage and even hatred. Anger is an impossible blockade on the road toward forgiveness. That blockade can be removed only when we surrender the underlying pain to God for healing.

God takes our pain on Himself, so use God as the lightning rod for your anger. The psalmists did exactly that in Psalms 7; 10; 17; and 28. Write out Psalm 10:17–18.

_____

_____

God alone is our avenger. Remember Job? There are dozens of places in the book where Job unloads his anger, frustration, and wounds onto God, along with a little sarcasm (Job 10:3). God can take all of those emotions and knows best how to handle them.

When someone wrongs us, instead of groping for a verbal weapon, reach for the Word of God: *"praying at all times in the Spirit, with all prayer and supplication. To that end, keep alert with all perseverance"* (Ephesians 6:18).

Instead of hitting our enemy, we can hit our knees. We can pray earnestly for God to heal our pain, remove our anger, and work forgiveness in us so we can extend it wholeheartedly to those who hurt us.

Instead of feeding our hurt, we can feed our heart. Relentlessly confess, repent, lay your hurt at His Table, and receive His forgiveness that refreshes.

God alone is our righter of wrongs. The power or responsibility does not lie with us. Write out what Scripture clearly tells us in Romans 12:19.

_____

_____

Never avenge yourselves. Forgiveness relinquishes all rights to punish our wounders and give them over to Christ. God is a God of justice as much as a God of love. Forgiveness does not mean that our wounders get off the hook; it recognizes that we are not the righteous judge of sin. That authority belongs to Christ alone.

Follow Jesus, not the path of revenge.

Drop the jawbone.

It stinks to high heaven.

Literally.

Pause
for Quiet Reflection

Intentionally schedule at least fifteen minutes of quiet time before the Lord with pen and paper in hand. Ask Him to still your busy mind and open your heart. Take your time reflecting on these questions, and then write down your answers.

1. **When you struggle with thoughts of revenge, how do you know when enough revenge is enough?**

_____

_____

2. Notice that Samson thought he had a "right" to carry out his own brand of revenge. He didn't like God's timetable or methods, so he took matters—and a donkey's jawbone—into his own hands. Revenge carries a lot of anxiety. The person is tightly wound or bound up with a hardened heart because he or she has no bigger sense of trust. Do you feel you have a "right" to revenge? Why or why not?

Apply
It Personally

Now that this lesson has provided some insight from the Word about the devastation that revenge can cause, review what you wrote in the Quiet Reflection section above. If you are practicing passive or active revenge against someone who has hurt you, take a moment to stop. Bow before the Lord in prayer, confess your anger, and ask Him to take that jawbone away. And when He does, ask Him to give you the strength never to pick it up again.

God has you in the palm of His hand as you walk through this study individually and together as a group. He promises to bring beauty from ashes, so keep walking.

♥

Small-Group Connection

As a group, take turns discussing some of the things you learned in the homework in Lesson 1.

1. In the introduction, what struck you most about the parallels between the sycamine tree and forgiveness?

2. What was the most meaningful discovery for you regarding what forgiveness is *not*?

3. We have all heard the phrase "If you haven't forgotten, you haven't forgiven." How has this lesson helped debug that damaging myth?

4. It's natural to harbor thoughts of revenge when someone hurts us. Why have you (or why have you not) dropped your jawbone?

Searching the Word Together

Look up and read aloud the following verses. Take turns discussing what strikes you most about each regarding forgiveness.
Ephesians 4:32
Colossians 3:12–13
Romans 12:17–19

Building Deeper Friendships

1. Since this is your group's first gathering as you start this study, pass around a sheet of paper and ask everyone to write down their phone numbers, home addresses, and email addresses.

2. Individually, take a minute to write on a piece of paper one sentence that reveals a belief that you have held about forgiveness that you now see may need to be altered in light of biblical truth. Pair up with one person in your group (preferably the same gender) and exchange papers. After reading each other's sentence, share how your sentence caused confusion or heartache in a relationship.

Praying as One

Gather back as a group and pray (either have one person pray or several as they feel led) that God will provide you the courage and strength to embrace the new things He is revealing to you about forgiveness.

Then in a moment of silence, ask each person to pray silently for the person with whom they exchanged sentences.

Going the Extra Mile

Studying a topic such as forgiveness can be a serious, painful business. It helps to be able to laugh. Sometime this week, buy a funny or wacky greeting card for the person with whom you exchanged sentences and mail it to him or her.

Remember to take time to laugh with one another to help prevent people in your group from becoming emotionally bogged down.

Lesson 2

FORGIVING FAMILY WOUNDS

One of the most powerful stories in Scripture that teaches us about forgiveness is the life of Joseph. We will cover many parts of his story throughout the rest of this study.

Joseph started out favored by his father and ended up second-in-command over Egypt. However, between those two points, Joseph suffered mistreatment, false accusations, loneliness, and undeserved punishment.

Enter the old saying "It's not how you start; it's how you finish."

Our choices make a difference.

Joseph was seventeen when his brothers sold him into slavery. Yet God's favor was on Joseph. The intelligent, handsome teenager was placed in Potiphar's house. Through hard work and honesty, Joseph proved worthy of more responsibilities. Potiphar soon placed Joseph in charge over all he owned (Genesis 39:2–6).

Just when Joseph's situation was looking up, Potiphar's wife made inappropriate advances toward him. When he fled from her, she falsely accused him of sexual misconduct. Upon hearing the news, Potiphar threw Joseph in prison, where he spent the next several years.

But God kept His eye on Joseph and granted him favor with the prison guards (Genesis 39:21–23). Following a series of divine events and dream interpretations, Joseph garnered Pharaoh's favorable attention. Eventually,

Pharaoh placed Joseph second-in-command only to himself over all of Egypt (Genesis 41:37–46).

Joseph was thirty when Pharaoh elevated him to that prestigious position. The choices that Joseph made during the time between prison and power made the difference between victim and victor.

Joseph clung to his faith and chose to trust God. Would you in similar circumstances?

When it was all said and done, Joseph forgave his brothers: "As for you, you meant evil against me, but God meant it for good, to bring it about that many people should be kept alive, as they are today" (Genesis 50:20).

Joseph recognized God's sovereignty in his life and saw that God had taken the wound that his brothers handed him and used it for good.

But there was a process involved that took many years.

Now that we know how Joseph's situation turned out, let's together look more closely at that process to discern how to apply God's Word and direction to our hurtful situations.

DAY 1:
FAMILY FEUD

So when Joseph came to his brothers, they stripped him of his robe, the robe of many colors that he wore. And they took him and threw him into a pit. The pit was empty; there was no water in it. (Genesis 37:23–24)

Joseph was one of two sons born to Jacob through his beloved favorite wife, Rachel. Jacob favored Joseph "because he was the son of his old age" (Genesis 37:3). Jacob even went so far as to make a beautiful coat of many colors for Joseph, but not for his other eleven sons, nine of whom were born to Jacob through his other wife, Leah, who was Rachel's sister, and through Leah's handmaid. Envy and sibling jealousy began to rear their ugly heads. You can almost see the DANGER AHEAD signs start flashing.

Joseph was handsome, intelligent, and more than a little spoiled. God began giving Joseph dreams that revealed he would rule over his brothers. How did Joseph's brothers respond in Genesis 37:8?

Foolishly, perhaps out of youthful enthusiasm, Joseph told his brothers about those dreams, which drove the wedge between his relationships with them even deeper. After all, who likes to be told he will bow down to someone he despises? Their hatred and jealousy of Joseph deepened.

Then one day, Jacob sent Joseph to spy on his brothers at work (see another flashing danger sign here?). The brothers reached their breaking point and hatched a plan to throw Joseph into a pit with the intent to kill him (Genesis 37:12–24). But Reuben spoke up to prevent the murder.

Judah suggested the brothers throw Joseph into the pit and then sell him into slavery. Secretly, Reuben planned to return to the pit to rescue Joseph before he was sold.

But before Reuben returned, the other brothers had sold Joseph for twenty shekels of silver to Midianite traders traveling to Egypt (Genesis 37:28). When Reuben returned to discover an empty pit, he assumed Joseph had been killed. The brothers took the robe, dipped it into blood, and took it to their father. Jacob mourned inconsolably (Genesis 37:34–35).

In many ways, for decades, Jacob had been too passive in properly shepherding his family. Perhaps Jacob's mourning stemmed from his realization that his favoritism toward Joseph contributed to his son's plight.

Family feuds are the worst. If you have influence over a child in some capacity, is there something you believe you have done that has caused adverse effects in his or her life? If so, what happened?

_____

_____

When it comes to family strife and pain, we can learn three helpful lessons from Joseph's situation:

1. No family is exempt from adversity. Although every family has its own version of *normal,* adversity is usually a part of it. We are fallen human beings, and we will not always get along—especially if we are confined to close quarters with a big family. I have three sisters, so growing up as one of four girls who shared beds, bathrooms, and meals, I can understand how day-to-day life can exhaust and frustrate even the most easygoing youngsters.

Joseph was one of *twelve* boys. I cannot even imagine the logistics of each day, much less how much time and effort it would have taken to keep the peace between different personalities. Adversity, whether great or small, is simply a part of family life.

2. No enemy is more subtle than passivity. Passivity avoids present issues that create future problems. Jacob was passive in disciplining his children. Learning from Jacob's example, Joseph's brothers were passive in their aggression toward their brother. But passivity can turn into violence when emotions are suppressed over long periods of time.

For instance, I do not like dolls. Period. They creep me out with their unblinking eyes and blank stares. My two youngest sisters had several dolls, including Barbies. My passive-aggressive way of coping with the creepiness was to take the heads off of their Barbie dolls and hide them. (I realize that Sigmund Freud would probably have a psychiatric heyday with that scenario.) But Mom and Dad did not put up with my behavior and intervened to put a stop to it. They made me apologize and instructed my sisters not to leave their dolls waiting for me at my bedroom's entrance.

Nowadays, my sisters and I reminisce and laugh at these early shenanigans. But we can laugh together only because my parents stepped in, brought the problem into the light, and dealt with it. I realize that may be a very small problem in light of your experience. But the bottom line is the same: family problems are best solved out in the open, where God's light and breath can bring healing.

3. No response is crueler than jealousy. Solomon said that jealousy is as cruel as the grave (Song of Solomon 8:6). He was right, of course. That green-eyed monster can convince people to act out in crazy ways. One day, Joseph and his brothers are eating around the dinner table, and then jealousy causes murderous thoughts the next. What does Proverbs 6:34 tell us?

_____

_____

The term "blind rage" came to mind with those verses. Ask God to weed jealousy out of your heart before it takes root and causes destruction.

Perhaps you have endured hardship or even abuse at the hands of family members. Chances are good you have heard some of this well-meaning advice from misguided believers:

- "He hit you? I can't even imagine! I'm so sorry, but God says you are supposed to turn the other cheek. God still commands you to submit to your husband."

- "Why do you keep remembering that old hurt? If you have really forgiven her, then just forget what she did. If you remember it, that means you haven't really forgiven her."

- "I understand that he keeps behaving badly when he drinks, but it shouldn't matter whether he apologizes to you. God says you are supposed to love him anyway and forgive him seventy-seven times."

- "Your father molested you when you were a kid. It's been fifteen years now, so just put it in the past! The Bible says you are supposed to honor your parents, so shelve the memories and move on with your life."

- "Are you still beating yourself up over what you did? Puh-lease! He deserved it and so much more. Just forgive yourself and get rid of the guilt!"

If you have been the recipient of such misguided advice, you know it only aggravates the wound. Family adversity cuts us to the core because families are the ones who should love us even when no one else does. Family is supposed to have your back even if the world turns on you. But that's not always the case, as we see in Joseph's family.

Joseph grappled with broken dreams and difficult life turns. As do we. But he kept his communication lines with God wide open.

That's the key.

Whether family or not, people will let you down because they are human. They will hurt you because all of humanity is broken. Yes, including you. Instead of listening to or heeding misguided advice, open wide the communication with God through prayer and His Word.

Faithfully keeping your eyes on God and moving toward forgiveness ensures that God will turn what people intended for harm and use it for your good and His glory.

Pause
for Quiet Reflection

Intentionally schedule at least fifteen minutes of quiet time before the Lord with pen and paper in hand. Ask Him to still your busy mind and open your heart. Take your time reflecting on these questions, and then write down your answers.

1. Is there a family wound that you are struggling to forgive? Please explain.

_____

_____

2. Based on what you've learned, how would you initiate the process of forgiveness with that person?

_____

_____

Apply
It Personally

Now that this lesson has provided some insight from the Word about forgiveness, review what you wrote in the Quiet Reflection section above. If the Lord has begun to change any of your previous beliefs about forgiveness reflected in your answers above, cross out the old words and write in new ones.

God has you in the palm of His hand as you walk through this study individually and together as a group. He promises to bring beauty from ashes, so keep walking.

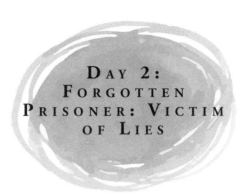

Lying lips are an abomination to the Lord, but those who act faithfully are His delight. (Proverbs 12:22)

Unjust suffering is one of the hardest trials we can experience. None of us escapes it. Every day, around the globe, reputations are ruined by malicious gossip, spouses are betrayed by adulterous partners, wives are mistaken for punching bags, and helpless children are sold as commodities.

The truth is that everything we hold dear can be taken away from us. Job is the perfect example of that. Yet we can hold on to our attitude and unwavering hope because God's love is guaranteed. The hope we have in Christ sustains us, lifts us up, and gives us a proper perspective. Where injustice occurs, our greatest test is our attitude toward those circumstances and holding on to the expectation that injustice will end.

What does 1 Peter 2:20 say?

_____

_____

Endurance is gracious in God's sight. As we continue looking at Joseph's life, his story continues with more injustices against him. After his brothers sold him into slavery, Joseph landed in Potiphar's house, where he worked hard and rose quickly to be appointed head over Potiphar's house.

Enter Potiphar's wife. She took a shine to the handsome young man and made inappropriate sexual advances toward Joseph. Wisely, Joseph literally ran from her. And though he fled from temptation and upheld his master's honor, he still suffered for it. At the speed of light, Joseph plummeted from the top of Potiphar's household into the depths of prison.

In such painful situations, we tend to ask, *"God, where are You?"* How does Genesis 39:21 answer that question?

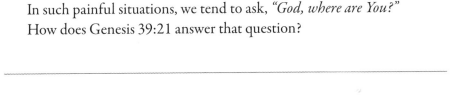

God is with us—*Immanuel.* When we wholeheartedly entrust our path to God and remain patient despite adversity, we become useful tools in God's hands. Our attitude makes all the difference.

Suffering injustice, particularly these three kinds, is common to everyone.

1. False accusations. James most appropriately describes the tongue as fire in James 3:5–6. In the blink of an eye, an untrue statement can incinerate a reputation that can take years to restore.

2. Circumstantial restrictions. We may be in a situation, either physically or emotionally, where we can't fight back or change the circumstances. Those constraints are painful.

3. Unwarranted mistreatment from family. Even in the most loving families, we eventually say or do something to hurt one another. Simply put: parents aren't perfect, and neither are children or siblings.

Are you experiencing any of these three scenarios? How are you working through it?

God's guidance is key. Attitude and intentionality play important roles in forgiveness. Here are five practices I have learned to adopt that will help you move toward forgiving those who commit injustices against you.

1. Worship. When we are in the Father's presence, hearing the Gospel proclaimed and receiving His gifts, His love, mercy, and forgiveness melt away all else.

2. Acknowledge that we all need forgiveness. Without Christ's work on the cross, we are just hopeless, helpless sinners. Ask the Lord to help you see them as a broken person, like us, who needs God's forgiveness. Receive the Lord's Supper. And be reassured.

3. Grieve over their sin. Yes, this is hard. Sometimes we can't see past the pain that their actions caused. Yet Jesus grieves over their sin and invites them back into relationship with Him. Ask the Lord to give you compassion to also grieve for their sins and pray that they move closer to God's grace and mercy.

4. Reach out to the one who wounded you. If it is safe for you to do so, prayerfully adopt a Christlike motive of seeking restoration (Matthew 18:15–17) and reach out to him or her. Remember, you can't make the other person receive your forgiveness. Your job lies only in faithfully extending it.

5. Search my heart, Lord. Am I trying to control the situation? Am I holding this person responsible for hurt that came in my past? Like David prayed in Psalm 139, ask God to search you and know your heart and then ask Him to keep searching it for any roots of bitterness that may be taking hold.

You cannot control how others treat you. But you can certainly choose how you respond. Your intentional, Christlike attitude of forgiveness will bear the fruit of peace and self-control in your life.

The next time injustice causes you to feel like a victim, remember that justice belongs to the Lord.

Jesus is trustworthy.

He will never forsake you.

He will never leave you!

Pause
for Quiet Reflection

Intentionally schedule at least fifteen minutes of quiet time before the Lord with pen and paper in hand. Ask Him to still your busy mind and open your heart. Take your time reflecting on these questions, and then write down your answers.

1. Sometimes it's too painful to name injustices—doing so makes them more real, more painful. But naming them is the first step in forgiving the people who committed them. What mistreatment or injustice have you suffered yet not fully acknowledged?

_____

_____

2. Imagine Joseph in that dark, lonely prison cell, shaking his fist in anger and crying tears of abandonment. Yet Joseph did not let darkness and loneliness become his social media tagline. Read Psalm 146:3–5. Those words are certainly reflected in Joseph's life. How can they also be reflected in your life?

_____

_____

Apply
It Personally

Now that this lesson has provided some insight from the Word about injustice, review what you wrote in the Quiet Reflection section above. Take this time to pray through Psalm 146:3–5 and ask God to make those things true in your life today.

God has you in the palm of His hand as you walk through this study individually and together as a group. He promises to bring beauty from ashes, so keep walking.

DAY 3:
RISING UP
PAST ADVERSITY

The Lord was with Joseph, and he became a successful man,
and he was in the house of his Egyptian master. (Genesis 39:2)

As you have studied on Day 1 and Day 2, Joseph was physically abused by his brothers. Jealousy consumed Joseph's brothers, and they literally threw him into a well.

And Joseph's long journey began.

His brothers sold him to human traffickers (Genesis 37), he was sexually assaulted by Potiphar's wife and falsely accused of rape, and he was eventually thrown into prison (Genesis 39).

In prison, he helped some fellow inmates (Genesis 40) who eventually betrayed him, forgot about him, and left him to rot in jail. For years.

So between the ages of seventeen and thirty, Joseph experienced one abusive situation after another. He was a victim to the whims of many. It's heartbreaking.

Yet there's more to his story. When Joseph was in Potiphar's house, he worked his way up and became head over Potiphar's household. When he landed in prison, he rose to a place of leadership and ran the prison under the supervision of the warden.

Joseph had a practice of rising up past adversity.

When adversity is in your life, do you have a habit of rising above it? Why or why not?

_____

_____

We see in Joseph's story throughout Genesis that the Lord was with him. The Lord is also with you. He gives you and me the strength to rise past any adversity.

When Pharaoh began having prophetic dreams, one of Joseph's former inmates remembered that Joseph could interpret dreams, and he told Pharaoh. Joseph was cleaned up and brought before Pharaoh. He interpreted Pharaoh's disturbing dreams, which prophesied a devastating famine (Genesis 41:1–31).

Joseph took his interpretation a step further and also provided to Pharaoh a crisis management plan to guide Egypt successfully through the famine (Genesis 41:33–36). Pharaoh liked Joseph's plan, placed him in charge of executing it, and promoted him to second-in-command of all of Egypt.

If we gloss over Joseph's story, it appears that he moved easily past those early abuses. However, if we pay attention to the details, we see that Joseph's journey toward forgiveness was a lot darker. And so is ours.

Forgiveness is not an easy process, but a necessary one.

The first sign that Joseph has not properly dealt with his past abuses surfaces when he later marries the Egyptian wife given to him by Pharaoh and they have two boys.

In Genesis 41:51, what does Joseph name his first son, and what does the name mean?

_____

_____

What does Joseph name his second son (v. 52), and what does the name mean?

_____

_____

By naming his sons that way, Joseph attempted to convey success— that he took terrible situations, overcame them, and rose up beyond them without ever receiving apologies from his past abusers. Some commentators interpret Joseph naming his son Manasseh to mean that Joseph is grateful to God that he ended up successful. For Ephraim, they interpret that God allowed Joseph to forget all that happened in the past and his father's house.

But perhaps that's not the whole story.

As we learned in Lesson 1, we can forgive deep hurts, but we cannot forget them. Ironically, Joseph, in naming his son Manasseh, guarantees that he will remember the past each time he calls out his son's name.

Although Joseph pontificates that God has allowed him to "forget" past abuses in his father's house, we don't see Joseph sending his dad a note letting him know he is alive. We don't see Joseph reaching out to his brothers to mend broken fences. As second-in-command of Egypt, Joseph could have easily sent messengers to his family. But he didn't.

If Joseph was suppressing anger, he operated in passive revenge.

Passive revenge is nonconfrontational and rarely involves the one who caused the offense. It touts an "I'll show you" mentality that attempts to substitute success for forgiveness. Although passive revenge is not outwardly destructive to our offender, it slowly destroys us from the inside out.

In the simplest of terms, Joseph basically named his first kid "Forget you" and his second kid "I win." What does that reveal about Joseph's level of forgiveness at that point?

_____

_____

Genesis 41:51–52 points to Joseph desiring to remember God's grace and mercy with his son's names. But for a person who does not know God's grace and goodness, those names conjure thoughts of past abuses and injustices suffered. Perhaps Joseph harbored bitterness and tried to pretend otherwise. Instead of extending honest forgiveness, maybe Joseph named his sons in such a way that guaranteed he would remember his family's past offenses until his dying breath. Instead of enjoying the success God provided, Joseph might have chosen to view his life through the lens of a painful childhood.

People who cling to unforgiveness build a self-made prison that eventually makes them invalids.

But when you and I, through the power of the Holy Spirit, confess bitterness and deliberately turn from it, we can embrace the process toward forgiveness. Then we can extend forgiveness to those who hurt us, and we are released from prisons of anger and bitterness.

Released not to merely exist.

Released to live *for* Him.

Enjoy life *in* Him.

Regardless of your past.

Pause
for Quiet Reflection

Intentionally schedule at least fifteen minutes of quiet time before the Lord with pen and paper in hand. Ask Him to still your busy mind and open your heart. Take your time reflecting on these questions, and then write down your answers.

1. **Like Joseph choosing not to let his family know he was alive and well, how have you seen old bitterness come out in your life?**

2. **If you are energizing your current success with the "I'll show them!" fuel, you will run out of gas fast. Truthfully, you may or may not see that person again. You can't *show* them. Then what?**

Apply
It Personally

Now that this lesson has provided some insight from the Word about rising past adversity, review what you wrote in the Quiet Reflection section above. All of us experience mistreatment and injustice at various times throughout life. Take a moment to remember how loved ones comforted and guided you during that vulnerable time. Write down some of the ways you receive comfort that you could pass on to the person who wounded you.

God has you in the palm of His hand as you walk through this study individually and together as a group. He promises to bring beauty from ashes, so keep walking.

DAY 4: HOW YOU CAN TELL IF YOU HAVE FORGIVEN

*If any of you lacks wisdom, let him ask God, who gives
generously to all without reproach, and it will be given him.*

(James 1:5)

I remember during times when I struggled to forgive, well-meaning Christians would tell me, "You just need to forgive." That's great advice, but exactly how was I supposed to do that?

When pressed for specifics, they would expound and say things like, "Forgiveness is not an emotion; it's a choice. You just choose to forgive." Okay, so I would declare to God, "I choose to forgive!" But the problem was that every time I thought of those who hurt me, it was like bile rising up in my throat. I would still relish thoughts about ways they needed to suffer. Not pretty, but real.

I knew that Scripture tells me to forgive, but I just didn't know how to get there.

When I confessed to friends that bitterness remained, they would say, "Forgiveness is just making the decision not to hurt them." Well, thanks, but I already made that call. I wasn't planning to hire assassins to hunt them down.

Despite their advice, my prayers, and searching Scripture, bitterness remained lodged in my heart. I could not find a way to dislodge it. Was I supposed to live with bitterness forever?

The incredible narrative in Joseph's story provides the answer. Joseph not only forgave his brothers but wholeheartedly did so. And we get to witness through the pages of Scripture how he eradicated that bitterness.

It is important for us to remember that these stories are not in Scripture to merely teach good lessons. These stories reflect a historical account of real people who faced difficult, real-life situations. Learning from these examples is vital to our spiritual growth.

Walking toward Forgiveness

When the famine in the land became severe, Joseph's brothers came to Egypt for food so their families would not die. Joseph recognized them, but his brothers did not recognize him (Genesis 42:1–8). After all, they had sold him into slavery over a dozen years earlier. He was probably dead, right? Also, Joseph likely looked Egyptian (shaving, dressing, and acting like an Egyptian).

So Joseph decided to test them to see if they were still the same cruel, self-centered men who had disposed of him long ago.

According to Genesis 44:1–13, how did Joseph test his brothers?

_____

_____

He tested his brothers to see if they would abandon Benjamin (Joseph's only brother who was also the son of Rachel) to starve and suffer. But then a beautiful thing happened.

In Genesis 44:18–34, what was Judah's response to Joseph's plan?

_____

_____

Judah revealed himself to be a man now marked with kindness and compassion. Judah was concerned for their father's well-being if they returned home without Benjamin.

Upon seeing this almost miraculous change in his brothers, Joseph revealed to them his true identity.

Read Genesis 45:1–15. What did Joseph tell them in Genesis 45:5–13?

_____

_____

How did Joseph's brothers react in Genesis 45:14?

_____

_____

The story of Joseph encapsulates a beautiful portrait of wholehearted forgiveness. God used Joseph's story to answer my lingering question about how to uproot the residual bitterness lodged in my heart.

Joseph effectively demonstrates the most helpful step we can take that creates space for God to remove unforgiveness from your heart: move toward the one who hurt you and wholeheartedly offer forgiveness.

Perhaps we need to pause here and ask ourselves why in the world we struggle so hard to forgive those who hurt us. The sin of withholding forgiveness is rooted in the brokenness of the world. It is rooted in original sin (thank you, Adam and Eve) and our sinful human nature. It's the proverbial devil on our left shoulder hissing in our ear that holding grudges feels good. Withholding forgiveness gives us a sense of revenge.

But those responses only hurt us. We often hear phrases such as, "She makes me so angry!" However, the truth is that we have chosen to feel angry. Unforgiveness and anger are feelings, and we can choose how we respond. God knows what is best for us, so we continue to confess, repent, receive His forgiveness, and walk in His strength.

By God's grace, I know what it feels like when God removes bitterness from my heart. I cannot properly articulate the complete sense of peace and freedom that I have experienced in those moments. Recognizing that God eradicates the roots of bitterness, walking toward those who hurt us to extend honest, deliberate forgiveness is the key.

How You Know You Have Forgiven

So, how do you know when you have arrived at forgiveness? As a card-carrying type A personality, I value progress. I look for markers of achievement in order to determine if my courses of action are working toward success. In my mind, success indicates goal achievement.

Several years ago, one of my pastors preached a sermon that beautifully clarified the sign of genuine forgiveness. He said, "You know you have forgiven when you are more sad at who that person has become than what they have done." Read that sentence once more. If you find that true of yourself, then God has already allowed you to forgive.

If you have been wondering how you know if you have truly forgiven, that's it. When you are more sad over who your offender has become than what he or she has done, you have forgiven. Yes, you will still remember the wound, especially when emotional shrapnel surfaces, but through forgiveness, you are no longer incapacitated by those wounds.

What a beautiful, redemptive affirmation of God's all-encompassing grace.

Pause
for Quiet Reflection

Intentionally schedule at least fifteen minutes of quiet time before the Lord with pen and paper in hand. Ask Him to still your busy mind and open your heart. Take your time reflecting on these questions, and then write down your answers.

1. **When you think of the person you are having difficulty forgiving, how did this day's study change your perspective?**

2. **As Joseph demonstrated, the key to eradicating bitterness from your heart is to walk toward the person who hurt you and offer forgiveness. Do you see that as a possibility in your situation? Why or why not?**

Apply
It Personally

Now that this lesson has provided some insight from the Word about getting rid of bitterness and understanding how you know forgiveness has happened, review what you wrote in the Quiet Reflection section above. Spend some time in prayer before God asking Him to reveal to you a way to test if the person who hurt you is truly repentant. Write down a plan, pray through it again, and step out to execute it.

God has you in the palm of His hand as you walk through this study individually and together as a group. He promises to bring beauty from ashes, so keep walking.

Day 5:
Canceling
the Debt

*God made alive . . . by canceling the record of debt that stood
against us with its legal demands. This He set aside, nailing it
to the cross.* (Colossians 2:13–14)

You have spent the last few days becoming familiar with Joseph's
story. He endured much pain and hardship at his brothers' hands.
Now, put yourself in the sandals of Joseph's brothers for a moment. They
had been invited into Joseph's presence, treated graciously, and given
bountiful provisions.

Their situation was looking up. Then Joseph decided to test his brothers.
What did he command the stewards of his house to do according to
Genesis 44:1–5?

_____

_____

Such a test may seem odd, but let's make this personal. If someone
has hurt or betrayed you, it is wise to determine if they have matured or if
they will inflict further harm. For example, if someone has betrayed your
confidence, it would be unwise to reveal your deepest, darkest secret before
determining whether that person would keep it confidential.

When Joseph's brothers sold him into slavery, they acted out of self-
centered jealousy (Genesis 37:11, 20). Joseph wisely decides to determine if
his brothers have cultivated mature, caring hearts.

In Genesis 44:6–13, what happened when the steward caught up with
Joseph's brothers and searched their belongings?

Upon finding Joseph's cup in Benjamin's possession, the brothers returned to the city to anxiously await Joseph's verdict. What would you be thinking at this point?

Without knowing Joseph's true identity or what he intended to do, the brothers were terrified. As second-in-command of Egypt, Joseph had the power to imprison them, make them slaves, or even put them to death. They fell to the ground before Joseph, hoping for mercy as Judah pleaded their case (Genesis 44:14–34).

Then in a flash of emotion, Joseph abruptly sent everyone out of the room and wept aloud. Fearing the worst, the brothers clammed up.

Joseph revealed that he was their long-lost brother whom they had sold into slavery more than a decade earlier.

How did the brothers respond in Genesis 45:3?

Their silence confirmed they expected their now-powerful brother to exact revenge.

Yet Joseph canceled their debts against him. Every. Single. One.

Their debts included the loss of family relationships and his years in slavery and in prison. How do you restore time to someone from whom you've stolen it? Yet Joseph absorbed them all.

The glory and splendor of Joseph's position are emphasized in Genesis 44. He could flaunt it and use it to control others. Yet, in humble modesty, Joseph unselfishly chose to share it with his brothers in all-encompassing reconciliation.

That's what Christ did for us on Calvary. He chose to humble Himself to descend to earth and share the magnificent glory of the Father with us—the sinful, guilty ones. Write out Philippians 2:8–10.

_____

_____

Christ absorbed our sin debt on the cross. Every. Single Bit. Of. It.

It is worthy to note that Joseph wisely forgave his brothers' transgressions in private (Genesis 45:1). You and I are urged numerous times in Scripture to follow suit. The fewer who are aware of the sin, the easier the offender can receive forgiveness instead of displaying false bravado. Write out Proverbs 10:12; 12:16; and 17:9.

_____

_____

When I struggle with canceling someone's sin debt against me, it's because I have lost sight of the massive, cavernous sin debt that God has forgiven in me. Martin Luther stated it best:

> Sins are forgiven in two ways: First, sin is driven out of the heart and grace is poured in; only God does this. Second, the forgiveness of sins is proclaimed; one man does this to another. Christ, however, does both. He puts the Spirit into the heart and outwardly proclaims it with words. . . . All people who are Christian and baptized have this power. In this way they praise Christ, and the words are put into their mouths, so that they can say, whenever they want and as often as it is necessary: "Look, dear man! God offers you His grace and forgives all your sins. Be comforted, your sins have been forgiven. Only believe it and you surely have it." . . . Thus in this way a Christian has the power to forgive sins.

Sometimes the opportunity to extend forgiveness takes a long time as people are separated by time and place. Yet if we have been offended, we stand ready to forgive and live our life as if forgiveness has already taken place.

Our key motivation is focusing on how God uses our tribulations to grow our faith. When our offender asks for forgiveness, we step forward to extend it and share how God used the incident for good.

There are four litmus tests you can take to determine whether you have forgiven your offender:

- **General thoughts test:** Can you think positive thoughts about this person? You've likely been in a close enough relationship with him or her to suffer such injury. Is there anything good about this person you can come up with? *If not, continue asking God to work forgiveness in you.*

- **Failure test:** When someone injures you, you can often wish harm upon him or her. Have you stopped looking for this person to fail? Forgiveness here means you would like this person to succeed or at least do better in life. *If not, continue asking God to work forgiveness in you.*

- **Revenge test:** Do you still think about ways to get even with this person? There may be consequences of his or her action that you must wait for, but even after those consequences occur, do you still desire to somehow make them pay for hurting you? *If so, continue asking God to work forgiveness in you.*

- **Opportunity to help test:** Would you help this person if you knew he or she were in trouble and you had the means and ability? I'm not suggesting that you subject yourself to further abuse or harm, but would you want this person to prosper or see him or her come to harm? *If harm, continue asking God to work forgiveness in you.*

Joseph passed all four of these litmus tests as he heard his brothers' genuine repentance.

If you are trying to determine whether you have canceled the debt of the person who hurt you, ask yourself those four test questions.

Your answers may surprise you.

Pause
for Quiet Reflection

Intentionally schedule at least fifteen minutes of quiet time before the Lord with pen and paper in hand. Ask Him to still your busy mind and open your heart. Take your time reflecting on these questions, and then write your answers.

1. **Which one of the tests mentioned in today's study can you not quite yet say "yes" to? I have failed all four at one time or another. It's beneficial to be honest with yourself so God can move you forward through the forgiveness process.**

_____

_____

2. **Do you doubt that you will ever pass all four tests? Why or why not?**

_____

_____

Apply
It Personally

Now that this lesson has provided some insight from the Word about canceling the debt of the person who hurt you, review what you wrote in the Quiet Reflection section above. Spend the next ten minutes in prayer asking God to reveal to you the tests for which you need His strength in order to pass. Then ask Him for the strength and wisdom to pass! Remember, specificity is the key.

God has you in the palm of His hand as you walk through this study individually and together as a group. He promises to bring beauty from ashes, so keep walking.

♥

Small-Group Connection

As a group, take turns discussing some of the things you learned in the homework in Lesson 2.

1. On Day 1, we dug into family feuds. Can you relate from your own family experience? What happened?

2. Being the victim of lies and a loose tongue can be harmful in every area of our lives, whether at home, church, or work. What about this lesson hit home for you? Why?

3. Even though Joseph ends up in atrocious circumstances, by God's grace he always rose above them. In Day 3, what tools did Joseph use to rise above his circumstances that you could use in your own life when adversity strikes?

4. It's hard to ascertain when you've forgiven someone. Do you experience a light-bulb moment or a feeling of peace? Explain why or why not. After reading that list, were you surprised that God has already helped you to forgive someone who hurt you?

Searching the Word Together

Look up and read aloud the following verses. Take turns discussing what strikes you most about each regarding forgiveness.

Proverbs 12:22
Colossians 2:14

Building Deeper Friendships

I have learned through wise pastors and Christian counselors that getting real about forgiveness means verbalizing it. Something happens when we articulate aloud how we're feeling or what we are struggling with.

Pair up with the person sitting across from you and risk sharing a specific challenge you're facing in a relationship with someone. If you don't have a current example, share one from your past and how you handled it.

Praying as One

Gather back as a group and pray (either have one person pray or several as they feel led) that God will provide you the courage and strength to embrace the new things He is revealing to you about forgiveness.

Then in a moment of silence, ask each person to pray silently for the person who risked and shared his or her story.

Going the Extra Mile

Sometimes, we are blind to the speck in our own eye when it comes to forgiveness. Are we contributing to the problem? Pair up with the person who shared his or her story with you.

Decide which of you will wear a blindfold. Have the other person pick out at item in another room. Now verbally guide that person to that object, making sure he or she doesn't run into something in the process! Ask your partner to describe it as best they can. Remove the blindfold and return to the group.

Discuss what that exercise taught about the importance of being able to see the speck in our own eye and the effects of spiritual blindness.

Lesson 3

FORGIVING BETRAYAL AND ABUSE

Forgiving those who betray and hurt us can be exhausting. During the process, we might be tempted to give up or look for an easy way out. During times when I have struggled to forgive, I remember asking God, "Does forgiveness have any loopholes?"

Over time and through much grace, God showed me what I was really asking: "Does Your *love* contain any loopholes?" You know, spaces where those imperfect people who hurt us deeply cannot be rescued. Places where offenders cannot be restored with His perfect love.

God's perfect love contains NO loopholes. Not for our offenders. Not for you. Not for me.

It seems easy to grab my offenders by the throat when I forget that I myself am a recipient of God's outrageous, scandalous grace—the same grace He unconditionally offers to them.

From a position of "wronged," I feel perfectly poised to play judge and jury over someone else's sin because, let's face it, I am convinced that someone else's sin is worse than mine.

But the truth is that God does not rank sin. Although not all sin carries the same consequences and the impact of sin varies, my offenses are no less offensive to God than anyone else's.

Write out Matthew 6:15 and Mark 11:26.

_____

_____

Jesus tells us to forgive or we will not be forgiven. It is not a divine guilt trip. Forgiveness is His grace-filled command to escape the spiritual hell of bitterness. His bidding frees us from the emotional torment that would otherwise bind us to our offenders forever because of their inability to pay their debts against us.

Betrayal and abuse cut us to the core. We struggle to pardon such atrocities.

But God's grace can pardon anyone.

It pardoned you and me.

Forgiveness for others' sins against us comes as we rest in God's pardon of ours.

That's not reasonable.

That's God's beautiful, unreasonable, life-giving grace.

DAY 1:
ADULTERY

It happened, late one afternoon, when David arose from his couch and was walking on the roof of the king's house, that he saw from the roof a woman bathing; and the woman was very beautiful. (2 Samuel 11:2)

He was supposed to be out with the army. That's what 2 Samuel 11:1 says about King David. But he decided to stay home.

He took a stroll along his rooftop and saw a beautiful woman taking a bath. David would have known she was in Uriah the Hittite's house, that she wasn't his for the taking. Upper-echelon officers were the ones who lived nearest to the palace. Such an arrangement kept the king safe from unknown assailants and officers out of trouble under the king's watchful eye.

And the rest, as they say, is history.

David lusted. Bathsheba succumbed. David had Bathsheba's husband murdered so he could marry her. They had a child. But God did not forget what took place. The price of David's sin was the life of their child.

So much collateral damage from one person who thought he was above reproach, the law, or reprimand. Are you and I any different?

Adultery plagues our world today. Whether we know a family member or friend who has suffered a wayward spouse, infidelity likely affects us all.

Teachers feel the effects in their classrooms when kids act out or their grades suffer as they process the emotional hurricane caused by their parents' divorces. Pastors' and counselors' schedules stay full as they walk the victims of adultery toward God's healing.

I don't use the word *victim* lightly. That's what adultery feels like. The one person to whom you opened your heart, body, and mind decided on some level that you were insufficient. Whether that insufficiency stems from within or is persuaded from without, it decimates intimacy.

Adultery ranks among the top significant hurts that are the most difficult to forgive. But that's not news. The real news is that "victim" is not our identity when we are in Christ.

What is your identity according to these passages?

John 1:12

_____

_____

1 John 3:1–2

_____

_____

Our identity is in Christ, so forgiveness is not optional. Forgiving the deep betrayal of adultery seems impossible. Have you experienced an unfaithful spouse?

If so, have you intentionally moved toward forgiving him or her? Why or why not?

_____

_____

It is perfectly normal to ask how you even begin such a daunting process. I asked that question several times. When our emotions are screaming for vengeance, entertaining thoughts of forgiveness seems impossible. But as God's children, we do not operate in our own strength.

What does Isaiah 40:31 say?

_____

_____

If you've experienced divorce, you will feel weary and faint. People question when I say, "Through gritted teeth, I asked God to forgive my ex-husband." That's because first and foremost, forgiveness is an intentional act of the will. When I kept asking God to help me forgive my ex-husband instead of dwelling on his actions, God focused my thoughts on Him. When we focus on the Lord and surrender toxic emotions to Him, He will set our heart right. Write out and ponder the following verses.

Colossians 3:2

_____

_____

Proverbs 3:6

_____

_____

What did the Lord reveal to you in those passages about forgiveness?

_____

_____

So how do you walk toward forgiveness? Begin with prayer. My prayers began with my asking God to heal my shattered heart and mend my broken spirit. Over and over and over. It was almost as if I needed to convince myself that I was worth such love. He did both and so much more.

Healing also took endless hours poring through Scripture. The verses God used powerfully in my life during that time were Psalm 18:16–19. Write them out here.

_____

_____

Did you notice God's action verbs? Take a moment to go back and circle them. Amazing! He sent, took, drew, rescued, brought, rescued, and *delighted*. Twice, He uses *rescued*. That's what it takes. *Relentless rescue is God's strong suit.*

No matter our hurt, its depth or its breadth, God rescues us. Why? Because "*He delighted in me.*" That's it. No other credential necessary.

Your worth is not stained by those who hurt you. Your lovability factor is not decreased by his or her actions. You are completely and wholly loved by God regardless of external circumstances.

When we endure painful seasons, knowing that Christ is our strength gives purpose to our pain. God never wastes a hurt. He will use that brokenness for our good and His glory.

Ask God to help you forgive your adulterous spouse. Keep asking. Not because God doesn't hear you, but to keep your focus on Him.

In Him alone, we find hope, healing, and the strength to forgive.

Pause
for Quiet Reflection

Intentionally schedule at least fifteen minutes of quiet time before the Lord with pen and paper in hand. Ask Him to still your busy mind and open your heart as you ask yourself these questions.

1. **If you have suffered the betrayal of an unfaithful spouse, have you begun to ask God to help you forgive him or her? Why or why not?**

2. **If you have been praying, how has God moved in your situation? Has He drawn your attention to specific Bible passages that will help you? If so, note those passages here.**

Apply
It Personally

Now that this lesson has provided some insight from the Word about how to walk toward forgiveness of an unfaithful spouse, review what you wrote in the Quiet Reflection section above. Spend the next ten minutes in prayer asking God for the strength to keep praying diligently to forgive your spouse (or ex-spouse) and the courage to allow God to heal your heart. Remember, specificity is the key.

God has you in the palm of His hand as you walk through this study individually and together as a group. He promises to bring beauty from ashes, so keep walking.

DAY 2:
SETTING
BOUNDARIES
AGAINST ABUSE

And I will betroth you to Me forever. I will betroth you to Me
in righteousness and in justice, in steadfast love and in mercy.

(Hosea 2:19)

Abuse is a heartbreaking reality in our fallen world. Some people see abuse on the nightly news. Some see it in their own homes.

First things first: if you are suffering severe emotional, verbal, or physical abuse in your current relationship, GET OUT NOW! Scripture does not teach that to be a forgiving Christian, you have to take a punch. Nothing could be further from the truth. We do see, however, numerous examples of setting boundaries to prevent abuse.

God Himself modeled good boundaries. Setting boundaries is a healthy exercise spiritually, emotionally, and physically—especially if the person you seek to forgive is an abusive person.

The Book of Hosea provides an appropriate scenario where God finally broke off His relationship with northern Israel because it would not turn from its evil, abusive ways. In showing how He dealt with a nation of abusers, God provides the perfect example of how to deal with our individual abusers.

Hosea provides detailed descriptions of the abuses Israel was guilty of, including cursing, lies, adultery, violence, and lack of love. Did you notice that those are the very behaviors we often see in domestic violence today?

According to Hosea 4:2 and 5:10, what does God say about northern Israel's violations?

We can use the steps God outlines in Hosea to draw boundaries with the abusers and boundary violators in our own lives.

Since God's very nature is love, it is sobering to see Him declare that He will no longer show His love to northern Israel (Hosea 1:6). Yet God still desires to restore His relationship with them (11:8–11). However, God withholds love and care in order to turn them from their destructive path and back to Him (2:9).

If you are dealing with an abusive situation, you may already have arrived at the stage where you are withholding love and care to let that person know they have violated your boundaries. Such actions may have improved the situation, but they may have also made it worse.

Hosea 2 outlines five specific steps God takes to address Israel's boundary violations, which lend invaluable, Christ-centered direction for your situation.

1. **Directly address and explain the boundary violation.** Christ-centered boundaries begin with speaking frankly about the issue, including expressing how a spouse's behavior is harming you and causing pain. Write out Hosea 2:2, 5.

_____

_____

2. **Outline and invite necessary behavior changes (Hosea 2:2b, 20).**

_____

_____

3. **State what you will and will not do.** Write out Hosea 2:6, 9, 21:

_____

_____

4. If necessary, set consequences (Hosea 2:3–6, 10–13).

_____

_____

5. If you wish to reestablish a relationship, set conditions under which that can occur. Write out Hosea 2:16, 20.

_____

_____

In Hosea 2, God shows that it is appropriate to end abuse, and He demonstrates how to set healthy boundaries. When you approach someone who has hurt you, they will either acknowledge the problem and offer to change, or they will resist.

The best scenario is that they admit they need to change, repent of their actions, and ask for your forgiveness. As God demonstrates, forgive them and reaffirm your love and commitment to that relationship. If possible, discuss the problem to see how you can help, and then agree on a follow-up plan if the situation does not change.

I learned in counseling that if the abuser resists, set respectful consequences designed to let that person experience some discomfort for their actions, including what action you will take if they violate your boundary again. The action establishes a boundary around you—the only person for whom you can take responsibility.

For instance, after my ex-husband's first affair, I established a boundary that if he ever strayed again, our marriage would be over. He violated that boundary with multiple affairs, so I enforced that boundary and sought divorce. Failing to enforce boundaries nullifies their significance and invites unchanged behavior to continue.

In Hosea, God draws this kind of boundary with Israel. Write out Hosea 5:15.

Out of love and mercy, God reinforces boundaries in order to restore a right relationship. He made it clear that He desired to show His love again once they ceased violating His boundaries.

However, in your situation it may be unsafe to confront your abuser. If you believe confrontation would legitimately jeopardize your safety, you may need to involve pastors, counselors, church friends, domestic violence counselors, law enforcement, or even a court of law.

In the midst of all of these steps and boundary discussions, the ultimate goal is forgiveness. It is imperative that we do not lose sight of that important goal. Regardless of what transpires, God commands us to forgive. Where continued abuse is involved, we forgive and keep the abuser behind a protective boundary.

Reconciliation is not always possible, but forgiving your abuser sets you free from bitterness and unforgiveness. If you have lived caged by fear, do not spend the rest of your life caged in bitterness. God promises you abundant life in Him.

Forgiveness allows you to *live*, secure in Christ and His plan for your life.

Pause
for Quiet Reflection

Intentionally schedule at least fifteen minutes of quiet time before the Lord with pen and paper in hand. Ask Him to still your busy mind and open your heart. Take your time reflecting on these questions, and then write down your answers.

1. **Can you think of a boundary violation you need to confront? Whom does it involve? What are the circumstances?**

2. How could you implement God's boundary steps demonstrated in Hosea to address the problem?

_____

_____

Apply
It Personally

Now that this lesson has provided some insight from the Word about setting boundaries against abuse, review what you wrote in the Quiet Reflection section above. Spend the next ten minutes in prayer asking God to bring the words to mind that He would have you speak to your boundary violator. As you seek His face, write what comes to mind.

_____

_____

God has you in the palm of His hand as you walk through this study individually and together as a group. He promises to bring beauty from ashes, so keep walking.

DAY 3:
OUR FORGIVING GOD

For You, O Lord, are good and forgiving, abounding in
steadfast love to all who call upon You. (Psalm 86:5)

Beginning with Adam and Eve's sin in the Garden of Eden, it is clear that only God can forgive sins. When God confronted Adam and Eve, the curse He spoke implied He would remedy the problem of man's sin through Eve's offspring. This offspring would eventually defeat Satan (Genesis 3:15).

Scripture repeatedly reminds us that God is the God who forgives sins. Read the following verses and write out God's posture toward forgiveness.

Exodus 34:5–7

_____

_____

Nehemiah 9:17

_____

_____

Psalm 130:4

_____

_____

Since we are all sinners, understanding that God forgives sin is important. The Bible recounts numerous stories of the devastating consequences of sin (Genesis 2:15–17; 3:22–24; Ezekiel 18:4; Romans 3:23; 5:12; 6:23; 7:14, 24; Revelation 20:12–15).

What we learn throughout Scripture is that God's forgiveness is the working out of His compassion and divine grace. God who forgives iniquity is also "merciful and gracious, slow to anger, and abounding in steadfast love and faithfulness" (Exodus 34:6).

He compassionately forgives those whom He chooses (Exodus 33:19). Based on our own merits or our own heart, we have no right to expect or demand His forgiveness.

But sin must be punished, so how can God's forgiveness be accomplished? Under Old Testament Law, men could offer sacrifices to God for their sins (particularly on the annual Day of Atonement, Leviticus 16:29–34). Under the new covenant, Jesus came to fulfill God's promise to forgive men's sins and to create in them a new heart (Luke 1:76–78).

When Jesus began His public ministry, it became clear early on that His mission on earth was to forgive sinners (Luke 5:17–26). When Jesus healed this man and forgave his sins, Jesus confirmed that He was the Messiah for eternal salvation for all who believe, for only He can turn the hearts of men toward God.

Through Christ's sacrifice on the cross, the forgiveness of sins was accomplished once for all. God did not overlook our sins, but punished them in His Son so that we might receive His forgiveness. That is the good news of the Gospel in a nutshell!

Along with forgiveness, God also granted repentance. Write out Acts 5:31.

_____

_____

When God brings sinners to repentance, two things happen. What is the first thing that happens according to the following verses?

Psalm 32:5–6

_____

_____

1 John 1:9

_____

_____

What is the second thing that happens according to the following verses?

Psalm 21:1–7

_____

_____

Psalm 51

_____

_____

Repentance means that we confess our sins and acknowledge our rebellion. Through the free gift of faith that God gives us in Baptism, you and I receive forgiveness of sins (Luke 7:48–50) by believing in the work of Christ on the cross as the full and final payment for our sins (Acts 10:43; Hebrews 9:11–10:18).

God operates daily in the forgiveness realm. He desires for us to receive His forgiveness and be restored aright with Him in all we do. He also desires for us to extend that same forgiveness to those who hurt us.

God's forgiveness is a one-stop shop: forgiveness for all who seek Him. Bar none.

Pause
for Quiet Reflection

Intentionally schedule at least fifteen minutes of quiet time before the Lord with pen and paper in hand. Ask Him to still your busy mind and open your heart. Take your time reflecting on these questions, and then write down your answers.

1. **What did you learn in today's passages about God's forgiveness that you haven't heard or studied about in-depth before?**

_____

_____

2. **In light of God's forgiveness for all who seek Him, does this change how you view the person(s) who hurt you?**

_____

_____

Apply
It Personally

Now that this lesson has provided some insight from the Word about our forgiving God, review what you wrote in the Quiet Reflection section above. Spend the next ten minutes in prayer asking God to remind you daily, if not hourly, that He is a God who forgives. He forgives you. And He stands ready to forgive those who hurt you. Remember, specificity is the key.

God has you in the palm of His hand as you walk through this study individually and together as a group. He promises to bring beauty from ashes, so keep walking.

DAY 4:
WHAT IF
THEY ARE
UNREPENTANT?

Come, let us return to the Lord, for He has torn us, that He
may heal us; He has struck us down, and He will bind us up.

(Hosea 6:1)

As God strengthens our faith and we grow in His grace, He molds us to be more like Jesus. And Jesus forgave.

But what if they did not repent?

One of Jesus' main teachings that we struggle with the most is that we are to love our enemies, pray for them, and even do good to them despite the pain they have caused. In our hurt, we can read the Gospels over and over and miss the point. We may grasp the theology but not the graciousness that Jesus taught and exemplified.

Imagine Jesus as He hung on the cross. How much repentance was demonstrated by those around Him? Not only was repentance absent among the soldiers who crucified Jesus, but contempt hung thick in the air. Yet what did Jesus say in Luke 23:34?

_____

_____

If Jesus would have adopted the position that His forgiveness should only follow repentance, He would have demonstrated that He was as lost as those He gave His life to save. He did not just pronounce His own forgiveness. He specifically prayed for *His Father* to forgive them. To forgive *us.*

My ex-husband was kind enough to tell me that I did not deserve how he had treated me by being unfaithful. And though I appreciated those words at the time, even had he not repented, I would still have been obligated to forgive him.

What does Jesus warn against in the following verses?

Jeremiah 7:13

Haggai 2:17

Matthew 11:20

Jesus is Lord over all, so we cannot choose whom we will forgive and not forgive. Judgment and consequences are up to the Lord. When we follow His command to forgive, we receive the blessing of living free of bitterness with no thoughts of revenge.

But what if those we need to forgive have died? They made you miserable while they were alive, and after death are unable to repent of their behaviors. Are we let off the hook to forgive? By no means. Forgiveness is a gift for *us*, remember? What then? We can show love and mercy to their families.

King David provides the perfect example throughout 1 Samuel. Even though King Saul tried to destroy David over the course of many years, David responded with kindness and forgiveness to the household of Saul.

After becoming king following Saul's death, David looked for anyone who was still living from the household of Saul so that he could demonstrate his love and friendship for Jonathan, Saul's son (2 Samuel 9:1). David showed kindness to the lame Mephibosheth by restoring to him and his family the land owned by the former king. David paid to have the land farmed and cared for and even made a place for Mephibosheth at his own table as an accepted part of the king's family.

Perhaps there is a Mephibosheth in your life to whom you could show love and kindness, despite how their loved one hurt you.

Whether or not the person who hurt you repents, forgiveness is still commanded. Not for their sake. *For yours.*

Pause
for Quiet Reflection

Intentionally schedule at least fifteen minutes of quiet time before the Lord with pen and paper in hand. Ask Him to still your busy mind and open your heart. Take your time reflecting on these questions, and then write down your answers.

1. **You might assume that the person who hurt you "should know what they did to you," but in actuality they might be clueless that they have hurt you. Have you directly approached the person who hurt you to let them know their offense?**

_____

_____

2. **If the person who hurt you has not repented, how have you responded so far?**

_____

_____

Apply
It Personally

Now that this lesson has provided some insight from the Word about forgiving the unrepentant, review what you wrote in the Quiet Reflection section above. Spend the next ten minutes in prayer asking God to soften your heart past your hurt and allow you to start the process of forgiving that person. Remember, your freedom and key to a new life, not theirs, is at stake.

God has you in the palm of His hand as you walk through this study individually and together as a group. He promises to bring beauty from ashes, so keep walking.

Know this, my beloved brothers: let every person be quick to hear, slow to speak, slow to anger. (James 1:19)

When Demi Lovato's album *Unbroken* was released several years ago, the album title intrigued me. I don't know much about Demi's history or music, other than her incredible vocal range. Yet I listened to the songs carefully to find out where she took the album's theme.

She wrote one of the songs to her dad, pleading for him to put down the alcohol and keep his selfish hands off his daughter. It broke my heart. How awful. Suddenly the stories that circulated on the Internet over the years about Demi entering rehab for cutting and bulimia made sense. Those behaviors are some of the ways people try to regain control over their lives because they have lived in an environment where they felt completely powerless.

So what does this have to do with anger? In the music video for that song, Demi demonstrates that she is using the power of success to overcome her painful past. (We also saw this behavior in Joseph's life in the Book of Genesis, remember?) Paraphrased, Demi's lyrics basically say, "Go ahead and try to tear me down, but I will rise from the ground like a skyscraper." It's a popular mind-set in our culture that says, "If you hurt me, I don't get angry and take revenge; I become successful to prove that you can't hurt me anymore."

However, such a mind-set is commonly driven by unresolved anger. We resolve to become indestructible skyscrapers, but have we dealt with what happened at the foundation?

How do the following passages describe God?

Exodus 34:6

_____

_____

Psalm 30:5

_____

_____

God set the example by being slow to anger. Anger is a volatile emotion that must be handled with kid gloves.

One day during my divorce process, I telephoned my television cable provider to switch the service from both of our names to mine only. The customer service representative could not seem to understand that my husband was unavailable to approve my request, even after telling her that my husband no longer lived in our home and would not be returning. I reached the breaking point. I shouted something about her being too deaf to hear and too dense to understand, slammed down the phone's receiver, yanked the whole thing out of the wall, and threw it across the bedroom with all my might. That was not a proud moment on many levels.

My over-the-top anger vividly taught me that anger can cause damage— literally. I asked God to remove those sharp, angry edges and begin the process of mending my heart. I prayed for that poor customer service rep whose hair I set aflame and asked God's forgiveness.

If you have struggled with anger, have you spent time asking God to remove it?

_____

_____

At one point during her video, Demi looks defiantly into the camera as if to say, "You tried to rip me down, but my sweetest revenge will be in-your-face success." That mind-set likely resonates with us at some level because all of us have been hurt. Whether someone betrayed a trust, shared a secret, or physically hurt us, we get it. We understand the need to prove that we can rise like a skyscraper above painful adversity.

But we will not find resurrection apart from Jesus.

Anger is appropriate if we've been hurt, but many of us take it further. Sometimes, we add coals of bitterness and resentment and stoke our anger with dreams of vengeance. But the truth is that we never master the flame. Fire doesn't work that way. It doesn't just scorch those who hurt you—it scorches *you.* Eventually, it will consume your life.

What does Psalm 37:8 say about anger?

_____

_____

Anger itself is not a sin. However, it may become sinful when excessive or prolonged. How does God instruct us to handle anger in the following verses?

Matthew 5:22

_____

_____

Ephesians 4:26

_____

_____

Colossians 3:8

_____

_____

When we hold on to anger and bitterness, the conflagration eventually destroys us from the inside out. Evil wins. So how do we properly respond to our wounds when we are surrounded by an outrage-obsession culture?

We don't resolve to throw telephones across the room or build skyscrapers.

We choose to forgive.

It is the only way to extinguish the flames of anger and once again put your feet on the path toward joy.

Surrender your anger to God.

Let Him build a skyscraper of grace in your life, built on the foundation of forgiveness.

Pause
for Quiet Reflection

Intentionally schedule at least fifteen minutes of quiet time before the Lord with pen and paper in hand. Ask Him to still your busy mind and open your heart. Take your time reflecting on these questions, and then write down your answers.

1. **If you have struggled with anger at the person who hurt you, reflect on how you have handled it so far. Have you given it to God or stewed in it? Explain.**

_____

_____

2. **Venting your anger is a one-sided speech, where calm confrontation invites dialogue. If you were able simply to vent your anger to that person, what would it help?**

_____

_____

Apply
It Personally

Now that this lesson has provided some insight from the Word about the damage that unresolved anger can cause, review what you wrote in the Quiet Reflection section above. Spend the next ten minutes in prayer asking God to reveal where your anger lies and what is at the root. Is it threatened security? Ask Him to move you from anger toward forgiveness. Remember, specificity is the key.

God has you in the palm of His hand as you walk through this study individually and together as a group. He promises to bring beauty from ashes, so keep walking.

Small-Group Connection

As a group, take turns discussing some of the things we learned in the homework in Lesson 3.

1. On Day 1, we dug into adultery and how that is one of the most significant hurts we are challenged to forgive. Can you relate and share wisdom with the group from your own experience?

2. Setting healthy boundaries to prevent abuse, especially physical abuse, is extraordinarily important. Where have you set up boundaries in your life? What prompted them?

3. On Day 4, we looked at forgiving those who are unrepentant. If you have experienced this challenge, what insight can you share?

4. We wrapped up this lesson by looking at the flames of anger and how they can prevent us from stepping forward to forgive those who wounded us. If you have experienced such anger, from where did it stem and how did God guide you through it?

Searching the Word Together

Look up and read aloud the following verses. Take turns discussing what strikes you most about each regarding our forgiving God.

Exodus 34:5–7

Nehemiah 9:17

Psalm 86:5

Psalm 130:4

Building Deeper Friendships

Forgiving betrayal and abuse leads to trust issues. The one(s) whom you thought you could trust with your most intimate thoughts and moments violated that trust. Pair up with the person sitting across from you and risk sharing with each other a specific challenge you're facing regarding trust. If you don't have a current example, share one from your past and how you handled it.

Praying as One

Gather back as a group and pray (either have one person pray or several as they feel led) that God will provide you the courage and strength to embrace the new things He is revealing to you about forgiveness.

Then, in a moment of silence, ask each person to pray silently for the person who risked vulnerability and shared their story with you.

Going the Extra Mile

When we have suffered betrayal and abuse, trust is the first casualty. Choose one person in the group who has admitted struggling with trust issues. Yes, it's time for that old trust exercise! Have the whole group stand behind that person. Ask that person to free-fall back into the arms of your group to remember what it feels like to trust. Don't you dare drop them!

Discuss what that exercise taught about the importance of being able to trust again, even though it has been a challenge based on past events.

Lesson 4

R E C E I V I N G   F O R G I V E N E S S

Not long ago, I watched an old movie titled *The Mission*. I am not necessarily recommending it because parts of it are violent. However, one overarching story line teaches a powerful truth about forgiveness.

The movie is set in the 1740s in South America. Young Robert De Niro plays a mercenary who makes his living by hunting down natives and selling them as slaves to the Portuguese and Spanish. He hones the necessary skills, which include shutting off his emotions and hardening his heart in order to function properly in the midst of such a dark profession.

However, De Niro's heart is open to love in one area: his little brother. He adores his little brother. But one day, De Niro discovers his brother and his own fiancée have fallen in love and are sleeping together. In a fit of rage, he loses his temper and kills his little brother. As his brother falls to the ground and breathes his last, you see it dawn on De Niro that he just destroyed the only source of love and joy in his life. In that moment, you see the guilt hit him like a wrecking ball.

The next time he appears in the movie, this hardhearted mercenary is curled up in a ball on the floor of a monastery, refusing to talk or eat.

His guilt has completely curled him into himself, and his only desire is to die. Then one priest approaches him and dares him to live. He reluctantly agrees but is still suffocating in the weight of his guilt.

One day, he accompanies the priests as they scale a mountainside to minister to some indigenous people at the top. As a self-imposed penance, De Niro chooses to fill a huge bag with weapons and carry it on his back as he climbs. Although the priests keep telling him that he is forgiven and free, he refuses to accept it. So he continues to claw and stumble up the mountainside, lugging that huge burden. At one point, one of the priests gets frustrated, cuts the bag off of his shoulders, and shouts at him that he does not have to carry such a burden. Yet De Niro retrieves the weight, straps it back on, and continues to climb, trying to earn forgiveness for his past atrocities.

Eventually, De Niro makes it to the top, and the very people he exploited, wounded, and hurt stare back at him. He kneels in front of them as they approach them with weapons drawn. One of the natives grabs him by the hair, puts a knife at his throat, and tells him that he deserves to die for killing and selling his people.

Then the man lets go of his hair, uses the knife to cut the ropes holding the burden on his back, and throws it over the cliff into the water below. All the people begin to laugh, because their tribe had become Christians. They had experienced the grace of God. So they forgave the man who had once been their enemy and called him a friend.

In that moment, as De Niro feels the burden of guilt fall from his back and as he receives the forgiveness from the very people he persecuted, he begins to weep uncontrollably. The laughing people surround him, patting his face and wiping his tears. Then he begins to laugh so hard that tears of joy mingle with tears of relief. The next time we see him, he is a missionary giving his life to love the very people he had hurt so terribly. Their forgiveness granted him the freedom to love again.

Sometimes, you and I carry our guilt like a burden on our backs. It weighs us down with regret, self-loathing, and shame. We beat ourselves up when we remember pain we caused or hurtful words we spoke. We replay the tape each day to pile up the guilt and shame that prevents us from embracing the freedom that Christ died to secure.

It's a picture of sin that Martin Luther called the incurvature of the soul, where a sinner's self-centered rebellion reaps the resulting predicament. Luther's first solution was the theology of the cross, which held that God manifests Himself so exclusively in suffering that no one can possibly seek Him in a self-serving fashion.

Christ's death and resurrection liberated us from the suffocating guilt and shame. Refusing to receive His forgiveness for ourselves is itself a sin. It sounds like humility when we say, "Well, you don't know what I've done. It's too bad to forgive." That's not humility; it is the sin of unbelief. The apostle John reminds us: "If we confess our sins, He is faithful and just to forgive us our sins and to cleanse us from all unrighteousness" (1 John 1:9). All means all. Christ faithfully cleanses *all*.

Sometimes, we are more readily inclined to forgive others before receiving God's forgiveness for ourselves. Yet God promises to forgive our transgressions and remember them no more. This lesson is one of the most crucial in this study. I pray that God opens your eyes and heart to the truth that His forgiveness is not only for those who hurt you, but it is also for *you*.

If You, O Lord, should mark iniquities, O Lord, who could stand? But with You there is forgiveness, that You may be feared. (Psalm 130:3–4)

We all commit mistakes that we believe are too big for God's grace, much less His forgiveness. When we mess up, there is a myth that often circulates among Christians as the truth. It goes something like this: "God has forgiven you; now you need to forgive yourself." Has someone ever said that to you?

It sounds like great advice, but it's a jail cell with no water.

This myth is a dangerous lie because it looks for healing in the last place we should look for it: ourselves. It assumes that God extends eighty percent of the forgiveness and it's up to you to muster the other twenty percent.

It's time to replace this dangerous myth with God's truth.

The truth is that you haven't believed and received God's complete forgiveness. We do not feel worthy of God's forgiveness, especially if our actions actively contributed to the pain inflicted—but that is what God's amazing grace is all about.

Forgiving ourselves is not only impossible, it is foolish, dangerous, and futile. It is a vain attempt of a soul plagued by guilt seeking relief from the very last place we should be looking: *ourselves.*

"Forgive yourself" is equivalent to telling a dying person, "Heal yourself." Like medicine, forgiveness comes from outside of us—from God, our healer.

Write out John 8:36 here.

_____

_____

Only the Son can truly set us free. Actually receiving His forgiveness despite our feelings of guilt is hard because it requires admitting sin. God knows no degree of sin. Whether we run a stop sign or run over a person, sin is sin. We are the ones who categorize sin.

God's truth reminds us that no matter what we have thought, done, or will do, God forgives us because of His Son's sacrifice on the cross.

God forgives you.

If you were the one who inflicted the pain, *God forgives you.*

If you ranted at the one who hurt you until your neck veins bulged, *God forgives you.*

If you're mad at God for your pain, *God forgives you.*

Although the hardest part about forgiveness is receiving it for ourselves, ponder this: Almighty God, maker of heaven and earth, creator of all things, has forgiven you, yet you cannot receive it for yourself? Again, we're trying to do God's job, and we stink at it. Forgiveness starts with embracing the truth and receiving God's forgiveness for yourself.

If you have trouble receiving God's complete forgiveness, pray for God to increase your faith to believe that truth. I cannot count how many times I have prayed that very thing.

What did the disciples ask Jesus in Luke 17:5?

_____

_____

We cannot forgive ourselves—that's God's job.

Hang on to this important truth: We are daily recipients of undeserved, baptismal grace in Christ Jesus. We have only to look at the perfect example of perfect forgiveness in Jesus—the sinless life, suffering, and death on the cross on our behalf. Once we understand that, we cannot help but share that grace with others.

God forgives, but we do not always receive and believe the light of truth. What does John 1:10–11 tell us?

_____

_____

Receiving God's forgiveness releases toxins from *your* mind and softens *your* heart to move freely into the future God has already planned for you.

The obstacles of shame and guilt erect barriers in our mind that cause us to believe that our past atrocities are beyond God's forgiveness.

Author Chad Bird beautifully describes guilt as our stalker:

> When the stalker appears, thrust toward her a thorn-crowned, blood-marked tree. She will fade into the darkness whence she came. She can do us no more harm, for her only weapon—our sins—have been ripped from her grasp by a nail-scarred hand. The ghostly lips that accuse us have been sewn shut by the one who, like a sheep that is silent before its shearers, was led as a mute Lamb to the saving slaughter. The chapters from our dark past have been expunged from the biographical record. They've been replaced by a single page from the Book of Life, in which our names are written in the ink of indelible, divine blood.

Receiving God's forgiveness allows us to move forward in life, fully free from guilt and shame.

And when the stalker comes knocking, reread Chad's quote.

Do that and receive God's forgiveness for yourself.

God has placed His amazing gift of forgiveness before you.

Open it and receive the beautiful freedom it brings.

Pause
for Quiet Reflection

Intentionally schedule at least fifteen minutes of quiet time before the Lord with pen and paper in hand. Ask Him to still your busy mind and open your heart. Take your time reflecting on these questions, and then write down your answers.

1. If you have caused the pain and hurt in someone's life, are you having trouble embracing God's forgiveness for yourself? Why or why not?

_____

_____

2. If someone has ever told you to "forgive yourself," how did that make you feel?

_____

_____

Apply
It Personally

Now that this lesson has provided some insight from the Word about the myth that we can forgive ourselves, review what you wrote in the Quiet Reflection section above. Spend the next ten minutes in prayer asking God to increase your faith so that you can receive His complete, grace-filled forgiveness for yourself.

God has you in the palm of His hand as you walk through this study individually and together as a group. He promises to bring beauty from ashes, so keep walking.

DAY 2:
WHEN GOD MEETS
YOU IN THE DIRT

*Jesus said, "Neither do I condemn you; go, and from now on
sin no more."* (John 8:11)

S he stood trembling before Jesus. Standing right in her own dirt as they
accused her. Eyes downcast. Shame creeping up red on her face. Fear
pounding her chest in waves. Here's how the story went:

> Jesus went to the Mount of Olives. Early in the morning He
> came again to the temple. All the people came to Him, and
> He sat down and taught them. The scribes and the Pharisees
> brought a woman who had been caught in adultery, and
> placing her in the midst they said to Him, "Teacher, this
> woman has been caught in the act of adultery. Now in the Law,
> Moses commanded us to stone such women. So what do You
> say?" (John 8:1–5)

That story causes me to cringe on many levels. But one thing blares
loud: *Don't we all have to face our own dirt sooner or later?*

Whether self-induced or coerced by others, sometimes we eat dirt over
poor choices. We try to hide them. But others find out. Haters yell it from
rooftops. Perhaps we believe that we deserve such treatment.

Maybe the woman did as well.

Condemned by her actions. Accused by her thoughts. Braced to endure
the harsh stones of judgment. *But landing in the dirt doesn't mean we have to
call it home.* The story continues like this:

> Jesus bent down and wrote with His finger on the ground. And
> as they continued to ask Him, He stood up and said to them,
> "Let him who is without sin among you be the first to throw a

stone at her." And once more He bent down and wrote on the ground. (John 8:6b–8)

Jesus refused to pick up a stone. And He blatantly challenged those who would. Scripture doesn't tell us where His gaze fell as He uttered those words.

Who would you be in this scenario? Some days, we crumple hard. Other days, we hurl thoughtless stones. But Jesus?

> But when they heard it, they went away one by one, beginning with the older ones, and Jesus was left alone with the woman standing before Him. Jesus stood up and said to her, "Woman, where are they? Has no one condemned you?" She said, "No one, Lord." And Jesus said, "Neither do I condemn you; go, and from now on sin no more." (John 8:9–11)

The older ones left first. I noticed that for the very first time when rereading these passages. The older had lived more of life. They knew how easily we can face-plant in the muck, how consequences can make your chest heave heavy.

Yet, Jesus didn't *condemn her. Or you. Or me.*

Time and again, Jesus faithfully picks us up, dusts us off, and sets us on the right path again. The only thing He asks in return? "Go, and sin no more." In other words, turn away from suffocating, dirt-inviting sin to breathe new life offered by Him.

This is a story of hope.

Jesus doesn't care what you've done. He doesn't care where you've been. *He cares about you!*

Jesus' question to the religious authorities and His answer to this woman delivered her from a terrible fate. After the people left, He expressed His unfailing love by not condemning her. His grace and kindness motivated the woman to take His words to heart.

What does 1 Peter 4:8 tell us?

_____

_____

When an offense has taken place, we need to constantly ask ourselves if love can cover it. Is there anything we can do or say that will prevent the hurt from escalating?

Jesus bent low to draw in the dirt, but His faithful, loving heart extended strong arms to lift her up. No stones. No condemnation. He does the same for you.

And our home?

It isn't in the dirt.

He's preparing mansions for us in heaven.

Talk about home sweet home.

Pause
for Quiet Reflection

Intentionally schedule at least fifteen minutes of quiet time before the Lord with pen and paper in hand. Ask Him to still your busy mind and open your heart. Take your time reflecting on these questions, and then write down your answers.

1. Have you ever felt like you sinned beyond Jesus's capacity to forgive? What were the circumstances?

---

2. Perhaps like the sinful woman, you have heard grace dropping around you like rocks. When you should have felt the pain, you felt His love. How has that affected how you extend forgiveness to others?

Apply
It Personally

Now that this lesson has provided some insight from the Word about Jesus's scandalous love in spite of our sin, review what you wrote in the Quiet Reflection section above. Spend the next ten minutes in prayer asking God to reveal those places in our life where we have landed in the dirt and forgiveness seems impossible. Take time to thank God for dropping grace like rocks into your life.

God has you in the palm of His hand as you walk through this study individually and together as a group. He promises to bring beauty from ashes, so keep walking.

See to it that no one fails to obtain the grace of God; that no "root of bitterness" springs up and causes trouble, and by it many become defiled. (Hebrews 12:15)

When Hurricane Ike carved a path of destruction straight through Houston in 2008, God provided me with an unforgettable mental picture of a root of bitterness. During the terrible storm, a huge, beautiful tree in my backyard ended up on my roof. When the storm passed, I hired a tree removal service to cut down what was left of the tree, leaving a nice, neat stump to sit on.

However, in the weeks that followed, mini-trees began sprouting all over the backyard. Each week new sprouts emerged, and each week I pulled them up. I could not figure out what was happening until a neighbor identified the problem. As long as the old tree stump remained, baby trees would continue to sprout from the live roots in a last-ditch effort to survive.

He referred me to a tree grinding service that spent all day grinding down the tree stump and the large, visible surface roots. The tree sprouts never reappeared.

The life lesson learned from that experience became vital to me. Despite pain and hurt in my past, I did not want anger and bitterness to sprout from the stump of unforgiveness and take root in my future. I called upon God through prayer and His Word to grind out those deep-seated roots. I did not want anger to germinate other areas of my life and cause damage in other important relationships.

By definition, bitterness is usually associated with anger and grudges that we allow to take root. God's Word provides clear insight and instruction about such roots in both the Old and New Testaments.

What does Deuteronomy 29:18 say?

_____

_____

This passage tells us that the root itself is not bitterness, but rather that it bears the poisonous fruit of bitterness.

Of what does Hebrews 12:15 remind us?

_____

_____

That passage does not specify whether the fruit is anger or unforgiveness, only that it defiles. Bitterness digs dark bunkers of anger far removed from the light and love of Christ. It begins as a seed planted in the soil of pain that takes root and bears deadly fruit. Since roots form underground, they are easy to hide and camouflage.

People who allow bitterness to take root may say they are fine. They may look fine on the surface, but their actions reveal the true story. Their angry words tell a different story as well, and it is easy to ascertain where these words are directed. For instance, anger at others sounds like, "They are a sack of poo." Self-directed anger sounds like, "I am a sack of poo."

As I travel to speak and teach from God's Word, I occasionally encounter people who have allowed old hurt to grow into roots of bitterness. It becomes evident in their callous tone, guarded conversation, and defensive words.

Hebrews 12:14–15 lends insight about roots of bitterness:

> Strive for peace with everyone, and for the holiness without which no one will see the Lord. See to it that no one fails to obtain the grace of God; that no "root of bitterness" springs up and causes trouble, and by it many become defiled.

Following peace becomes difficult when we are preoccupied with babysitting our angry roots to ensure they remain buried.

God can and will eradicate those roots of bitterness from our life when we trust Him with the grinder. The process is painful, but necessary. And the result is a smooth landscape—a clean heart—ready for God to plant new growth and opportunities in your life.

Pause
for Quiet Reflection

Intentionally schedule at least fifteen minutes of quiet time before the Lord with pen and paper in hand. Ask Him to still your busy mind and open your heart. Take your time reflecting on these questions, and then write down your answers.

1. **Do you recognize callous tones or guarded words in your conversations regarding a certain topic or person? If so, when and with whom?**

_____

_____

2. **If you answered yes to that question, chances are you have a root of bitterness in your heart or mind. When did it start?**

_____

_____

Apply
It Personally

Now that this lesson has provided some insight from the Word about roots of bitterness, review what you wrote in the Quiet Reflection section above. Spend the next ten minutes in prayer asking God to identify any roots of bitterness in your life. Ask Him to remove them completely from your life. Remember, specificity is the key.

God has you in the palm of His hand as you walk through this study individually and together as a group. He promises to bring beauty from ashes, so keep walking.

DAY 4:
WHEN YOU CAUSED THE WOUND

So if you are offering your gift at the altar and there remember
that your brother has something against you, leave your
gift there before the altar and go. First be reconciled to your
brother, and then come and offer your gift. (Matthew 5:23–24)

We learned in Lesson 1 that forgiveness means to excuse a fault or offense and to absolve from payment of. But what if you were the one who inflicted the damage?

It's inevitable in our fallen world and busy schedules. We act before we think and sometimes hurt those we love most. Sometimes, those acts are intentional and sometimes not, but regardless of intent, the resulting hurt is real.

So when we are the offenders, what do we need to do to repair the damage? What answer does God provide in Matthew 5:23–24?

_____

_____

Notice that the verses do not say that you have something against your brother, but instead that your brother has something against *you*. Regardless of how big or small the offense, these passages clearly line out the steps we are to take:

1. **We are to make amends urgently.**

God even goes so far as to instruct us to leave our offering at the altar and approach the person whom we hurt. He says, *leave your gift . . .*

and go (v. 24). We are His priesthood of believers, and God is our priority. However, God realizes the importance of community and desires us to repair relationships with those around us without delay.

2. **We are to repent and forgive one another immediately.**

Why the haste? People know that we are Christ followers by His love that shines through us. When we harbor unforgiveness or hurt, people see discord and animosity instead of His love.

Also, we do not know what tomorrow holds. What does 1 Thessalonians 5:1–11 tell us about the urgency of time?

_____

_____

Then Matthew 5:23–24 goes on to say that *after* we have reconciled with each other, *then* we are to present our offerings to Him. In other words, if we have hurt or offended someone, we are to drop everything, humble ourselves, repent before God and the one(s) we offended, ask for forgiveness, and make restitution.

Only when we have obeyed can we return to God's altar to offer unimpeded worship and enjoy fellowship with Him.

The beautiful truth of the Gospel is that when we repent and ask for God's forgiveness, He forgives and cleanses.

Write out 1 John 1:9.

_____

_____

What if those you have hurt will not forgive you for the damage done? It is not our job to make someone accept our relationship-restoring effort. Our job is to offer honest, wholehearted repentance. We must trust God to do the rest.

When we keep short accounts with one another regarding wounds inflicted, the sooner we can get back to the beautiful picture of the fellowship portrayed in Acts 2:42–47. What are the believers doing in those passages?

_____

_____

I don't know about you, but that is a beautiful picture of God's people my heart longs to see across the globe.

That is a community welcoming to all.

Pause
for Quiet Reflection

Intentionally schedule at least fifteen minutes of quiet time before the Lord with pen and paper in hand. Ask Him to still your busy mind and open your heart. Take your time walking through these steps:

1. **Do you believe the pain or hurt you inflicted on that person is beyond God's ability to heal?**

2. **Confess out loud to God the actions that damaged the other person.**

3. **Ask God out loud to forgive you for your actions and to bring healing to the person who was hurt.**

4. **Pray out loud for as long as it takes. Doing so allows God the space to cleanse your conscience and lift the burden from your heart.**

Apply
It Personally

Now that this lesson has provided some insight from the Word about the importance of restoring relationships when we have wounded someone, review what you wrote in the Quiet Reflection section above. Now, let's make this personal:

- Stand before a mirror, *look yourself in the eye* (yes, it can be hard at first), and tell yourself *out loud*: "God has forgiven you. You are cleansed and purified based on the truth of His Word. You *are* forgiven. Receive it!"

- Repeat this process every day until the truth of God's promise brings you peace. Do not forget to look yourself straight in the eye!

God has you in the palm of His hand as you walk through this study individually and together as a group. He promises to bring beauty from ashes, so keep walking.

DAY 5:
AS FAR AS THE EAST IS FROM THE WEST

As far as the east is from the west, so far does He remove our transgressions from us. (Psalm 103:12)

This verse became real to me when I first heard the beautiful song "East to West" by Casting Crowns. I had never given much thought to the distance between east and west, because it is an exercise in futility. We may as well try to measure how long, wide, high, and deep is God's vast universe.

East to west finds no end, and neither does God's loving, infinite forgiveness for us. God desires for us to have an intimate relationship with Him. It is precisely for that reason that God sent Jesus to live the perfect life we could not and take upon His shoulders the wrath for every sin we have ever or will ever commit.

In the midst of pain, God's forgiveness shines forth like a life raft on a dark ocean of deadly waves.

Because Jesus volunteered to pay the wages of our sin, God has forgiven us. What does Romans 6:23 affirm?

_____

_____

As we learned in Lesson 3, Day 3, our God is a forgiving God. But not only does God forgive our sins, He also forgets them and does not hold them against us. How do you see this truth in Isaiah 43:25?

_____

_____

We learned on Day 1 that you and I cannot forgive ourselves. We do not have power to erase our memories. So God determined to forget our sin to restore relationship with us. Write out Hebrews 8:12:

_____

_____

The Bible emphatically states God's willingness to forgive. This is especially important if you tend to be a people pleaser or a perfectionist. We are human. We live in a fallen, post-Eden world. It is inevitable that we will make mistakes. Jesus knows we cannot be perfect. But He asks us to be present and fully engaged and rejoicing in the life our Creator so generously gives us. If we hesitate to engage because we are afraid of messing up, we're not really living.

The forgiveness God bestows on us means He

- does not punish for our sin (though we may feel its consequences);

- fully and completely restores our relationship with Him;

- does not love us less;

- does not hold our sin against us in future actions; and

- does not speak ill of us.

When we realize how completely God has forgiven us, and continues to forgive us, it is truly unthinkable to harbor feelings of unforgiveness against others.

As far as the east is from the west, God removes our transgressions. Not just forgives them, but _removes_ them.

This does not mean that God simply ignores our sins. Our sin is an offense to a holy and just God. Our sin is an open rebellion against God, where we are telling God that our happiness, convenience, and preferences are more important to us than He is. We are guilty and deserve His judgment.

Only God can erase our sins or cleanse our hearts. That is precisely what God did when He sent our Lord Jesus Christ here to die in our place. We deserve death, but Jesus took all our sins upon Himself and died in our place. Because of that immeasurable grace, our sins have been forgiven.

Through the faith that God gives us, we can repent and turn our hearts toward Him. Our sins are gone! We are washed clean by the blood Jesus shed for us.

Our resurrected King is determined to resurrect you.

Pause
for Quiet Reflection

Intentionally schedule at least fifteen minutes of quiet time before the Lord with pen and paper in hand. Ask Him to still your busy mind and open your heart. Take your time reflecting on these questions, and then write down your answers.

1. **What struck you most from the lesson about the depth and completeness of God's forgiveness for you?**

2. **In light of God's example, what can you learn to apply in forgiving those who hurt you?**

Apply
It Personally

Now that this lesson has provided some insight from the Word about how far God removes your transgressions from you, review what you wrote in the Quiet Reflection section above. Spend the next ten minutes in prayer expressing gratitude from a thankful heart that God has indeed removed your sins and remembers them no more. Remember, specificity is the key.

God has you in the palm of His hand as you walk through this study individually and together as a group. He promises to bring beauty from ashes, so keep walking.

Small-Group Connection

As a group, take turns discussing some of the things you learned in the homework in Lesson 4.

1. On Day 1, we talked about the myth of forgiving yourself. How did God change your perspective with the truth that the real issue is receiving His forgiveness?

2. Like the woman who committed adultery, we sometimes land in the dirt because of our actions. But Jesus forgave the woman, and her accusers dropped their rocks. In the same way, Jesus has also forgiven you. Tell of a time in your life when you heard God's grace drop like rocks when you believed punishment was coming.

3. Roots of bitterness can be hard to eradicate once they have taken root. What was most helpful to learn about allowing God to grind them out of your life?

4. On Day 4, we studied how hard it is to know that you have wounded someone. What steps toward seeking forgiveness and reconciliation prove to be most helpful?

Searching the Word Together

Look up and read aloud the following verses. Take turns discussing what strikes you most about each regarding our forgiving God.

Hebrews 8:12

Hebrews 12:15

John 8:9–11

Building Deeper Friendships

Consider the astronomical cost Jesus paid to dwell in intimate fellowship with us. We can only imagine how He must grieve when we allow our shame and guilt to keep our relationship with Him at arm's length. Instead of dropping our rocks at His holy quarry, where He grinds every boulder of sin with His grace, we choose to carry our rocks. Pair up with someone in your group, and tell him or her which internal enemy you struggle with the most, whether shame, guilt, or something else. Determine the size of your rocks and ask God for the strength to leave them at His quarry for destruction.

Praying as One

Gather back as a group and pray (either have one person pray or several as they feel led) that God will provide you the courage and strength to receive His forgiveness.

Then in a moment of silence, ask each person to pray silently for the person who risked vulnerability and shared his rock story with you.

Going the Extra Mile

Commit in this week ahead to hunt for rocks as a group or with a few close friends. Pick a place where you are likely to find a variety of stones. Choose several different rocks of varying sizes and shapes and each of you make a pile. Mentally name the rocks in your pile: guilt, shame, pride, stubbornness, and so on. Then one by one, have group members pick up each rock and with one voice of confidence yell, "Jesus forgave this!" and drop those rocks never to be picked up again.

FORGIVING REPEATED OFFENSES

I don't want to become a Christian doormat." We usually hear that phrase when a repeated offender enters our life. That statement is usually followed with questions such as, "Am I supposed to forgive every time even though they won't stop?" "Am I setting myself up as an easy target for them to take advantage of me?"

Somewhere along the line, Christians allowed a skewed picture of instant, easy forgiveness to mingle with God's truth.

Jesus hits the issue of repeated offenders head-on in Luke 17:3–4: "Pay attention to yourselves! If your brother sins, rebuke him, and if he repents, forgive him, and if he sins against you seven times in the day, and turns to you seven times, saying, 'I repent,' you must forgive him."

I have heard Christians sometimes paint the forgiveness canvas with only one stroke labeled "forgive immediately without question." Frankly, that sentiment leaves us feeling frustrated and victimized as easy prey.

Sin breaks fellowship, first with God and then with one another. Repentance means to turn away from sin, which is an integral part of the forgiveness process. When Jesus instructed Peter to forgive seventy-seven times, He was referring to *the same sin.* In other words, repeat offenders.

Repeat offenders litter Scripture. Remember Hosea's wife? What about Saul's vengeful behavior toward David? If you are a repeat offender, you are not alone.

We will spend time in this lesson looking at forgiving repeated offenders. But let's start by getting real. We all fall into that category, don't we? I sure do. I have offended people at work, home, and even church. Although most were unintentional, close proximity to the same people is a breeding ground for repeat offenses—whether given or received.

But God never leaves us without hope. If you are a repeat offender or have been repeatedly offended, I pray that this lesson lends valuable insight into forgiving all and moving through life breathing the fresh air of unencumbered freedom in Christ.

Forgiveness should be enthusiastic, lavish, eagerly offered, and unrestricted—even for repeat offenders.

After all, every one of us is a repeat offender against God.

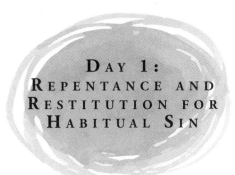

For godly grief produces a repentance that leads to salvation
without regret, whereas worldly grief produces death.

(2 Corinthians 7:10)

When it comes to repeated offenders in our relationships with others, forgiveness is linked with repentance and restitution. Many questions revolve around those sensitive issues, so we will address them individually in the context of Scripture.

Repentance vs. Apology

True repentance always involves two key components: a confession of wrongdoing and a willingness to make things right. Conversely, an apology frequently takes the form of an excuse.

In fact, the word *apology* comes from the Greek *apologia,* which translated means "a speech in defense of." Apologies equate with self-defense, usually noted by the word *but*. For example, "I am sorry if my actions offended you, *but . . .*"

Repentance is a genuine admission of wrongdoing and a request for forgiveness. For example, "I did not realize that my comment offended you. It was unintentional and thoughtless. Will you forgive me?"

Genuine repentance involves heartfelt sorrow before God for our sins and prompt action with the one we offended in order to correct them.

True repentance is a rare thing to find, even in the Bible. But we find it in David after he commits adultery with Bathsheba and then orders the murder of her husband, Uriah.

Read 2 Samuel 12:1–13. What indicates that David is truly repentant?

_____

_____

David further expands his confession in Psalms 32 and 51 regarding this same sinful behavior. Read through those psalms and write down the phrases that indicate David's repentance is genuine.

_____

_____

David's real repentance is revealed by his admission of sin (2 Samuel 12:13; Psalm 32:3–5). David rightly and appropriately acknowledged he had sinned against the Lord *first* and others *second*. David's painful process of repentance climaxed when Nathan confronted him about his adulterous behavior.

Did you notice that as long as David kept silent about his sin he was in agony? When God's Spirit indwells a believer, sin grieves the Spirit and takes no pleasure in it (Hebrews 11:25).

David expressed his repentance through unqualified confession of His sin before God, and then he took his sin seriously. Psalms 32 and 51 show that David pondered the weight of his sin, and the longer he pondered, the more atrocious it became.

We need to take note of an important example set by David regarding sin: God does not grade on a curve. That false assumption leads believers to attempt to offset their sins with good deeds. If they deem themselves to be more good than bad, they do not grasp the quality of righteousness God requires.

What does James 2:10 say?

_____

_____

When someone approaches you using apologetic language in place of true repentance, beware of their sincerity. We can confess our wrongdoing and still not genuinely repent of it. Therefore, when you approach someone whom you have offended, be careful to approach them with genuine repentance and not apologetic excuses.

What goal did Jesus specifically state in Luke 5:31–32?

_____

_____

Repentance restores relationships—us with God and then us with others. Apologies only drive the wedge of separation wider.

Biblical Restitution

Anyone can accidentally hurt us or commit a onetime sin, but when it comes to repeated offenders, repentance and restitution go hand in hand.

The biblical concept of restitution is supported by both the Old and New Testaments. At its core, restitution removes the profit from sin. It serves as a deterrent to repeat offenses.

Restitution means the act of returning what was wrongfully taken or replacing what was been lost or damaged. Obviously, restitution is much easier when our loss is tangible. But restitution becomes nearly impossible when the collateral damage is shattered trust.

God forgave us our sin debt but did not do so until Jesus made restitution for those sins by sacrificing His life. When someone asks for our forgiveness but is unwilling to make biblical restitution, their sincerity becomes suspect.

In order to grasp biblical restitution, read Exodus 22:1 and 22:3–6, 14. What are the key components of restitution according to those passages?

_____

_____

In the New Testament, Zacchaeus was a prominent repeat offender. Because of his past, Zacchaeus offers a perfect example of restitution. Take a moment to read Luke 19:1–10. What phrases offer clues that Zacchaeus repented with a sincere desire to make restitution?

_____

_____

We can gather from Zacchaeus's words that he admitted his guilt in defrauding people, his remorse, his public confession, and his promise to Jesus to make restitution. That, friends, is genuine repentance.

Those same principles hold true for believers today. True repentance creates a desire to make right what we have done wrong, as much as possible. Admittedly, there are some sins for which adequate restitution does not exist. In those instances, we cannot hold on to guilt for the inability to make full restitution.

Restitution is not a requirement for salvation; rather, it is a result of it.

When you receive the forgiveness of sins through faith in Jesus, *all* of your sins are forgiven—whether or not full restitution can be made.

Believe it by faith.

Receive it with humility.

Live it in love.

Pause
for Quiet Reflection

Intentionally schedule at least fifteen minutes of quiet time before the Lord with pen and paper in hand. Ask Him to still your busy mind and open your heart. Take your time reflecting on these questions, and then write down your answers.

1. If you have a repeat offender in your life, what signs have they exhibited that point to genuine repentance and restitution?

_____

_____

2. If you are the repeat offender, have you expressed true repentance and moved toward making restitution? Why or why not?

_____

_____

Apply
It Personally

Now that this lesson has provided some insight from the Word about repentance and restitution, review what you wrote in the Quiet Reflection section above. Spend the next ten minutes in prayer asking God to reveal to you any areas in your life where you need to step forward and offer true repentance and restitution to someone. Then ask God to open opportunities for it to come to fruition.

God has you in the palm of His hand as you walk through this study individually and together as a group. He promises to bring beauty from ashes, so keep walking.

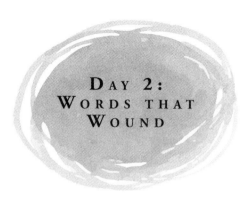

DAY 2:
WORDS THAT
WOUND

Having a good conscience, so that, when you are slandered,
those who revile your good behavior in Christ may be put to
shame. (1 Peter 3:16)

Sometimes, well-meaning friends put their foot in their mouth. It's just part of life. But then there are those people whose intentional cruel comments cause deep wounds.

When someone you love hurts you deeply—especially if they are close to you or fellow Christ followers—the last thing you desire to be is civil to them. If you were blindsided, the offense hurts more. Your natural self-defense mechanisms kick in, and you want to lash out and hurt them as much as they hurt you.

Although spilling ugly words may feel good for an instant, it proves extremely harmful in the long run. There are two things we can never recover: wasted time and hurtful words.

Taking the High Road

Each conversation we have with those who hurt us can go either of two ways: productive or destructive. We have to remember that every time we communicate with people who have hurt us.

I have learned to continually ask God to give me words of grace whenever I communicate with someone who has hurt me. Perhaps you are in such a place with someone close to you. Some days you just want to spew poisonous words. But once they've been said, you can't unsay them.

What do the following passages tell us about how we are to speak to one another?

Proverbs 16:24

_____

_____

Ecclesiastes 5:2–3

_____

_____

Matthew 15:11

_____

_____

Those passages can be hard to read when we have been hurt. Have you ever lost your temper and said ugly words to someone who has hurt you? What happened?

_____

_____

Oftentimes, the self-loathing we feel after verbally shredding someone who hurts us is simply too high a price to pay. Perhaps we feel momentary satisfaction if we rant, spew curses, and call them names, but how many of those names would be true of us under different circumstances? God always shows grace, and as you saw in the verses above, He teaches that His children are to act likewise.

Jesus' Words Communicated Grace

As God's children, we are bound to express lavish, grace-filled forgiveness. Even when it hurts most. As Jesus hung on the cross as the innocent sacrifice for our sins, He prayed for you and me, *"Father, forgive them, for they know not what they do"* (Luke 23:34).

I have often used Jesus' prayer for those who hurt me: *"Father, forgive him, for he knows not what he does."* Sometimes, I have prayed those words through gritted teeth. But I learned firsthand that you cannot pray for someone without God changing your heart. Eventually, God allows us to pray forgiving words with genuine care and concern. God's pretty amazing like that.

Taking the high road in communicating with someone who hurt you may result in biting your tongue until it's bloody. But it means we will have obeyed God's command to forgive and this added benefit: you can look in the mirror without regretting ugly words spoken.

Write out these additional verses about how we are to communicate with one another.

James 3:9–10

\
\

Ephesians 4:15

\
\

Yes, always climbing to the higher road can get exhausting, but it's an exercise toward your freedom. You have the strength to make this climb, step by step, by the power of the Holy Spirit that dwells in your heart. You are baptized and redeemed. You wear the yoke of your Savior, Jesus Christ. The ability to sleep peacefully knowing you honored God with your words and actions is priceless.

Words that wound can echo long in your heart and soul. Keep seeking God and His peace that passes all understanding. He never disappoints.

Remember, the person who hurt you is also someone Jesus died to forgive and restore.

Pause
for Quiet Reflection

Intentionally schedule at least fifteen minutes of quiet time before the Lord with pen and paper in hand. Ask Him to still your busy mind and open your heart. Take your time reflecting on these questions, and then write down your answers.

1. **If someone you love dearly has spoken words that wounded you, have you spoken with him or her? If so, what was the result? If not, why not?**

_____

_____

2. **Sometimes, it helps to journal what you need to say to someone who has hurt you before you actually talk with that person. Bring to mind the person whose words have hurt you. What would you say? Do your words line up with the Bible passages from this lesson?**

_____

_____

Apply
It Personally

Now that this lesson has provided some insight from the Word about words that wound, review what you wrote in the Quiet Reflection section above. Spend the next ten minutes in prayer asking God to remove the sting of those hurtful words from your heart and mind. It is not a selfish prayer; it is a necessary prayer in order to move toward forgiving the person who hurt you. Remember, specificity is the key.

God has you in the palm of His hand as you walk through
this study individually and together as a group. He promises
to bring beauty from ashes, so keep walking.

Day 3: The Spiritual Warfare Factor

In all circumstances take up the shield of faith, with which you can extinguish all the flaming darts of the evil one; and take the helmet of salvation, and the sword of the Spirit, which is the word of God, praying at all times in the Spirit, with all prayer and supplication. (Ephesians 6:16–18)

As God's beloved children, you and I are engaged in spiritual warfare against an unseen enemy, wearing unseen armor, in a culture that doesn't even acknowledge the raging battle.

But engaged we are.

Flip on the news. Scan your computer's home page. Notice the conflict in our relationships. The evidence is present in spades.

We are soldiers in a spiritual war that started in the Garden of Eden and will continue until Jesus Christ returns. Satan and his demonic army represent our enemy, whose ultimate goal is our complete and utter destruction. Cunning, deceptive, and deadly, Satan deploys every conceivable weapon, ignores polite rules of engagement, and lies to accomplish his goal.

Scary? You bet.

We battle good versus evil, right versus wrong, and God's light versus Satan's darkness all the time! But God does not leave us defenseless. He provides us His armor to prevail. In His Son, God has provided everything needed for us to proclaim ultimate victory over unforgiveness and bitterness.

What do the following verses reveal about how and what God provides?
Philippians 4:19

_____

_____

Luke 12:31

_____

_____

Psalm 84:11

_____

_____

Yet some Christians choose to ignore the raging spiritual battle because of fear. They refuse to stand and defend their post because the reality that a powerful, unseen enemy actively labors to destroy them seems too frightening to bear.

What does God tell us about fear?
Psalm 46:1–2

_____

_____

2 Timothy 1:7

_____

_____

God has *not* given us a spirit of fear! When it comes to forgiving those who repeatedly wound us, we may fear that our temper will get the better of us and permanently damage our relationship with them. Well, that is certainly a possibility. However, this perspective may help you as it did me.

In the pain of our woundedness, sometimes we lash out against human opponents as though they are the enemy. But understand this truth: Satan uses human beings as tools to stir up bitterness and unforgiveness. Beyond those who would harm us, we will see the real foe who lurks in the shadows.

We end up wasting time and energy fighting one another rather than fighting the real enemy who seeks to control people and lure them to oppose God's command to forgive.

In Ephesians 6, Paul describes open warfare with flaming darts—a frightening scenario where we smell the smoldering swaths of destruction torched by the enemy, who delights in watching lives and relationships go down in flames.

The ancient flaming arrow, or fire dart, was traditionally made of cane with a flammable head. Once lit, it was shot in order to set fire to wooden shields, cloth tents, and anything else it pierced.

The enemy's use of fire depicts his goal of complete destruction. Fire brings annihilation to the point of being unrecognizable. This represents Satan's ultimate goal for a Christian's life. Perhaps the one who wounded you is a dear friend or loved one. Sometimes, that person becomes so completely deceived by the enemy's lies that you cannot even recognize his or her actions and words. You find yourself taking a step back and trying to find the same person you once knew. It's stunning to say the least.

Maybe you have been that person whom others no longer recognize. The good news is that we don't have to remain unrecognizable. Falling toward God and into His light, love, and grace restores us. We are *never* out of reach of His redemption.

The enemy's fiery darts can never burn us beyond God's recognition and restoration.

Christ Jesus lovingly resurfaces our hearts and minds with grace and mercy as He removes our soot-stained garments.

Since unearthly fire tips the devil's arrows, only a divine shield quenches them promptly. The shield of faith extinguishes all the doubts, whisperings, and evil suggestions of unforgiveness.

God gives us His shield of faith to catch those arrows to present them back to our Commander in Chief. We extract those burned darts out of our shield and lay them before God as a sacrifice of praise.

In the spiritual warfare of forgiveness, it is not that we didn't take a hit; rather, we praise Him because *His* shield of faith provided the protection we desperately needed against a hardened heart. In the following verses, how does God shield us from the enemy's attacks?

Deuteronomy 11:25

_____

_____

Deuteronomy 28:7

_____

_____

Joshua 1:5

_____

_____

Joshua 21:44

_____

_____

These verses strengthen and encourage God's warriors. That's you and me. Warriors, not wimps.

So the next time someone you love dearly holds on to unforgiveness, peer beyond them into the proverbial shadows to find the real enemy. Forgive the one who hurt you, and hold God's shield of faith up to the enemy who instigated it.

Holding on to that thought helps us to keep a right perspective on the real enemy. When we struggle to forgive someone who hurt us, we can acknowledge our own sin against God, confess, and rush to make things right with the one who hurt us. Sometimes, we may need a counselor, mediator, or pastor to begin that necessary journey, but moving past the enemy on the battlefield to face the one we need to forgive is imperative.

And perhaps that repeat offender will eventually allow God to transform him or her into a wonderful peacemaker.

Step out in faith, and watch Him work wonders.

Pause
for Quiet Reflection

Intentionally schedule at least fifteen minutes of quiet time before the Lord with pen and paper in hand. Ask Him to still your busy mind and open your heart. Take your time reflecting on these questions, and then write down your answers.

1. In what kinds of situations do you find yourself fearful?

_____

_____

2. The enemy uses the hurtful things of the world to lure us away from God's command to forgive. He carefully observes us to find our weaknesses, and then he pounces when we least expect it. How do you see that reflected in your life?

_____

_____

Apply
It Personally

Now that this lesson has provided some insight from the Word about our very real spiritual warfare, review what you wrote in the Quiet Reflection section above. Spend the next ten minutes in prayer asking God to identify where in your life and relationships the enemy's flaming darts are aimed at right now. Ask God to send His quenching water to put out those darts and usher in forgiveness and reconciliation.

God has you in the palm of His hand as you walk through this study individually and together as a group. He promises to bring beauty from ashes, so keep walking.

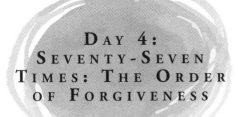

Pay attention to yourselves! If your brother sins, rebuke him, and if he repents, forgive him, and if he sins against you seven times in the day, and turns to you seven times, saying, "I repent," you must forgive him. (Luke 17:3–4)

Luke 17 begins with Jesus teaching His disciples about faith, duty, and the temptations to sin. Then, abruptly in the middle of His discourse, He forcefully reminds the disciples, *"Pay attention to yourselves!"* (Luke 17:3).

Jesus clearly points out that every believer shoulders responsibility for shepherding fellow believers away from sin and for being ready to forgive, just as God through Christ's loving sacrifice forgave us.

When it comes to sin, it's human nature to pay attention to others' missteps. We can easily fall into the habit of abandoning meaningful relationships in order to critique other people, judge their motives, and react accordingly. We often become hypersensitive to offenses.

Such a posture does not allow enough space for us to focus on our own path, our own sin, or our need to seek forgiveness from those we offend.

In today's culture, it has almost become standard procedure to act outraged over other people's faults in order to steer attention away from our own.

But this behavior is not new. It has been going on since the beginning of time. In Genesis 3:12, we read of the first instance of blame-shifting. When God asked if Adam and Eve had eaten the forbidden fruit, Adam started pointing fault at the woman "whom You gave to be with me." Then Eve joins the blame game and defends herself by shifting blame to the serpent (v. 13). And remember David's fiasco with Bathsheba? When Nathan told David a fictional story about a rich man who took a poor man's only beloved sheep for his dinner, David became outraged.

Write out David's reaction from 2 Samuel 12:5–6.

Nathan then rebukes David that he, in fact, is that rich man from the story because he took Uriah the Hittite's only wife, Bathsheba, for his own. It's easy to demand someone's head for a wrong done until we look in the mirror and see that it is our own.

What does Matthew 7:3–5 teach us?

In His Sermon on the Mount, Jesus warns against judging others. Luke 17 is a perfect example of making sure we pause before we point out the mistakes and flaws of those around us. In fact, Luke 17:3–4 outlines four specific steps to follow when someone sins against us:

1. **Rebuke the offender.**

2. **Allow space for repentance.**

3. **Forgive if they repent.**

4. **Repeat as long as that cycle continues.**

Theologians have engaged in much heated discussions through the years around that third point. Does Jesus really mean to forgive *only if* someone repents? Some people use this passage to staunchly withhold forgiveness until the offender repents. However, such narrow logic directly opposes Colossians 3:13, as well as other passages.

What does the Lord command in Colossians 3:13?

_____

_____

As we learned in previous lessons, God's command to forgive is not a suggestion, nor is it contingent on a human being's repentance. As Christ followers, we forgive as the Lord forgave—completely and without hesitation. Period. Now if the person genuinely repents, it certainly makes extending forgiveness a tad easier. But as we studied in our last lesson, repentance has many faces and levels of authenticity depending on the contrition of the offender.

So if you withhold forgiveness until you feel that your offender has repented _enough,_ you may be stalled in a toxic brew of unforgiveness for the rest of your earthly days. That's _exactly_ what God does _not_ want you, His child, to experience.

Did you notice that Jesus specifically refers to the number seven in Luke 17:4? The number seven in Scripture often means totality or perfect completion. Here our Lord makes it clear that seven does not necessarily signify a literal number, but rather the overarching figure of totality.

There are seven days in a week, and all of time is encompassed within the number seven. So when Jesus said, _"If he sins against you seven times in the day"_ (Luke 17:4), He meant that regardless of what our offender does or how he or she sins against us, we are to extend forgiveness.

Jesus answers Peter in a similar way in the Book of Matthew.
Write out Matthew 18:21–22.

_____

_____

Here, Jesus goes so far as to say _"seventy-seven times."_ That does not mean we are to count to seventy-seven transgressions against us and then quit forgiving offenses. The number is representative of the totality of forgiving those who hurt us—it is unlimited.

Peter likely thought he was being generous by offering seven times, but Jesus takes it much further in order to convey continuous action.

But let's bring this discussion home. We have difficulty forgiving someone a single trespass, much less seven. And seventy-seven? When someone sins and causes us pain, we may want to return the favor. But that's not what God commands.

You may be tempted to tell anyone and everyone about how you've been wronged—except the one who inflicted it. But actively engaging in gossip does not fall within the parameters of shepherding fellow believers away from sin.

What does the Eighth Commandment state in Exodus 20:16?

_____

_____

Gossip interferes with the forgiveness process by injecting doubt and further hurt. Jesus set the forgiveness bar high and rightfully so. He gave His life so that we could experience forgiveness from the Father and one another. To take that responsibility lightly disgraces His sacrifice.

It may sound morbid, but envisioning Christ on the cross each time I have a choice whether or not to forgive hurtful actions by a repeat offender helps me walk faster toward forgiveness. And every time I received the Lord's body and blood at His Table, He strengthened me for that walk.

We do not want to degrade our Lord's sacrifice by withholding the forgiveness He died to give. Perhaps keeping such a mental picture handy might help you as well.

Seventy-seven times is a tall order to fill.

But Christ's Spirit filling us provides the strength and power to fill that order every single time.

Pause
for Quiet Reflection

Intentionally schedule at least fifteen minutes of quiet time before the Lord with pen and paper in hand. Ask Him to still your busy mind and open your heart. Take your time reflecting on these questions, and then write down your answers.

1. Do you have a chronic, repeat offender in your life? If so, have you followed the steps of forgiveness outlined in Luke 17:3–4? If not, how can you intentionally try them in the future?

2. When it comes to forgiving a hurt, do you intentionally wait to extend forgiveness until your offender repents? Why or why not?

Apply
It Personally

Now that this lesson has provided some insight from the Word about unconditional forgiveness, review what you wrote in the Quiet Reflection section above. Spend the next ten minutes in prayer asking God to give you the tenacity and strength to follow His forgiveness guidelines when repeat offenders hurt you. Ask Him to keep His sacrifice that enables forgiveness at the forefront of your mind each time you are wounded. Remember, specificity is the key.

God has you in the palm of His hand as you walk through this study individually and together as a group. He promises to bring beauty from ashes, so keep walking.

DAY 5:
WHEN WE REFUSE TO FORGIVE

Then Peter came up and said to Him, "Lord, how often will my brother sin against me, and I forgive him? As many as seven times?" Jesus said to him, "I do not say to you seven times, but seventy-seven times." (Matthew 18:21–22)

In the passage above, Peter believes that he has shown generosity. After all, forgiving someone who sins against us is hard. But forgiving seventy-seven times? We learned about that in yesterday's lesson. Let's take time today to dive a little deeper.

Within Judaism, what do the following verses reveal about a forgiving spirit?

Job 33:29–30

_____

_____

Amos 1:3

_____

_____

Amos 2:6

_____

_____

Three times were sufficient to show a forgiving spirit. With the rule of three in mind, Peter believes he has offered more than double the normal amount. Generous, right?

Not according to Jesus. His answer reveals that true disciples are to forgive without keeping count. Jesus immediately launches into a parable. He relates a story (Matthew 18:21–35) about a servant who owed his king an exorbitant debt of ten thousand talents, which translates to about six billion dollars in today's currency. The king ordered that the servant, his family, and all he owned to be sold to repay the debt (this was a common practice in that era—see Exodus 21 and Leviticus 25). The servant threw himself on the mercy of the king, who pitied him and forgave *the entire debt*.

Now the unforgiving servant had a fellow servant who owed him a hundred denarii, which was about one hundred days wages—a very small amount compared to the six-billion-dollar debt the unforgiving servant had just been forgiven.

The unforgiving servant demanded that the fellow servant pay the debt in full, even going so far as to grab and choke him. No mercy, no compassion. When the indebted servant could not pay and instead begged for mercy, the unforgiving servant mistreated him, ultimately throwing him in prison until he could pay the debt. Ironically, the unforgiving servant put the indebted servant in a situation where he would never be able to repay the debt.

Other servants observed what had happened and relayed the story to the king. How did the king respond according to Matthew 18:32–34?

This story is a dramatic illustration of the massive sin debt we owe to our holy, righteous God. Like the forgiven servant, we have no hope of ever repaying our colossal debt. The wages of sin is death (Romans 6:23). So God graciously provided Christ's death and resurrection to pay our debt and break the power of sin in our lives. We partake in that death and resurrection through Baptism. And we receive the benefits of it every time we partake of the Lord's Supper. Christ frees us once and for all.

The image of being released from a debt is the perfect illustration of what it means to forgive. Since God extends unlimited forgiveness, the lesson is that we are to do likewise. Since the audience for this parable is Peter and his companions, it specifically addresses believers.

There are a few interesting points that we cannot miss in this parable. The unforgiving servant had amassed an *insane* amount of debt. I'm not quite sure how one goes about accruing a six-*billion*-dollar debt, even if you bought the most expensive estate, fifty Rolls Royces, and ten yachts. It shows the reckless nature of the unforgiving servant.

The unforgiving servant also never admitted his inability to repay. In fact, he actually said that he would pay it off. Not that he *could*, but that he *would*. There's a vast difference between reality and intentionality. It demonstrates how little he appreciated his own forgiveness.

Then the unforgiving servant turned around and refused to forgive another servant of a *much smaller* debt. We are so much like this servant. We don't like letting someone who hurt us off the hook. But in not forgiving, we (like the unforgiving servant) put ourselves in God's place.

He then sent his fellow servant to prison, where he could not repay the debt. This is important because no one can ever repay you for harm done. The damage has been inflicted. We can make amends, but we can never erase what happened.

When someone injures me, he or she incurs a debt. I have a choice of how to handle that debt. I can get mad. I can say that I forgive, but I harbor resentment. And I can demand repayment *or else*. But each of those answers creates misery. *For me.*

The point is this: God's forgiveness of our enormous sin debt provides our motivation to extend forgiveness to all who hurt us. I can never repay God for the sin debt I owe. Likewise, those who hurt us can never repay the debt they create in us. The damage is done. But we can forgive and move back toward trust.

Forgiveness releases the other person's debt against me and releases the judgment and consequences over to God.

As God's children, we are expected to pay forward His immeasurable gifts of grace and mercy. The gift of Holy Baptism washes us clean and makes us God's children.

God forgives us so much more than we will ever be asked to forgive.

Pause
for Quiet Reflection

Intentionally schedule at least fifteen minutes of quiet time before the Lord with pen and paper in hand. Ask Him to still your busy mind and open your heart. Take your time reflecting on these questions, and then write down your answers.

1. **Read the entire parable of the unforgiving servant in Matthew 18:21–35. What parts of the parable is God highlighting in your mind regarding His command to forgive?**

_____

_____

2. **How does this parable affect the way you view the massive sin debt God has forgiven you?**

_____

_____

Apply
It Personally

Now that this lesson has provided some insight from the Word about what happens when we refuse to forgive, review what you wrote in the Quiet Reflection section above. Spend the next ten minutes in prayer asking God if there is anyone in your life right now from whom you are either consciously or unconsciously withholding forgiveness. Ask God to set your feet on the path toward releasing that debt and forgiving them. Remember, specificity is the key.

God has you in the palm of His hand as you walk through this study individually and together as a group. He promises to bring beauty from ashes, so keep walking.

♥

Small-Group Connection

As a group, take turns discussing some of the things we learned in the homework in Lesson 5.

1. On Day 1, we talked about restitution. What new insights did God provide for you about that biblical principle?

2. Many people do not take spiritual warfare into account when they are struggling to forgive someone who hurt them. Oftentimes, we do not recognize the real enemy is in the shadows pulling the puppet strings. How did this lesson provide a new perspective for you?

3. On Day 4, we looked at the order of forgiveness found in Luke 17:3–4. Reread those passages and share which of those steps you find the hardest to take.

4. On Day 5, we wrapped up Lesson 5 by looking at the parable of the unforgiving servant. In light of the sin debt that God has forgiven you, how does that perspective help you to forgive others their sin debt against you?

Searching the Word Together

Look up and read aloud the following verses. Take turns discussing what strikes you most about each regarding our forgiving God.

Luke 5:31–32
Matthew 18:21–22
Ephesians 4:15

Building Deeper Friendships

At one time or another, each of us struggles with someone who is a repeat offender. Whether intentional or not, they seem to hurt us in some way more often than others. Pair up with someone in your group, and each of you identify your repeat offender to the other. Share a brief summary of how your repeat offender has hurt you. Then write his or her name on a small slip of paper. Exchange slips of paper with your partner and commit to pray for each other's repeat offender each day for the next week. Ask God to move in those repeat offenders' lives in such a way as to change their behavior based on God's love for them instead of mere obligation. When you gather again, be sure to share if God gave you any insights about your repeat offenders to share with one another.

Praying as One

Gather back as a group and pray (either have one person pray or several as they feel led) that God will see clear to remove repeat offenders from your life.

Then in a moment of silence, ask each person to pray silently for the person who risked vulnerability and shared his or her repeat offender's identity with you.

Going the Extra Mile

It is beneficial to remember that we are embroiled in spiritual warfare—especially where relationships are concerned. We need God's shield of faith to extinguish the enemy's fiery darts. This week, make a note of every time you believe the enemy has launched a fiery dart at you. And as the week progresses, write how God extinguished it. At your group's next gathering, share a few from your list with the group. When everyone has finished sharing, pray for God's continued protection for each of you in the ongoing spiritual warfare.

Lesson 6

Forgiving Injustice and Persecution

It was 1:30 p.m., and I was already fed up. The day had been crazy busy at the law firm where I worked. Clients were pacing in the conference room. Opposing counsel and his client paced in an adjacent one. All nervously awaited the mediator's decision on their respective proposals to determine whether the huge litigation would settle or be forced to go to a full, expensive trial.

The partner I had just been assigned to work for had a temper, and he loved to shout. Colorful words often peppered his outbursts. I was not a fan of his rants, but they were usually directed elsewhere, so I learned to tune them out.

Except on that day.

In the midst of the settlement negotiation hustle and bustle, he needed to sign important papers in a different case to extend a mandatory court deadline. I knew it was a distraction he would not welcome, but a court deadline was not something to take lightly.

I chose a moment when everyone seemed to have calmed down and poked my head in his office. I felt the tension in the room but pressed on. I walked the papers to his desk, completely unprepared for the response I received.

His face turned beet red, and his neck veins bulged as he lit into me for having the nerve to interrupt him. During his rant, he knocked over a full cup of coffee onto the papers. I turned, walked out of his office, and left for the day after letting the office manager know why.

Later, I could hardly remember exactly what he said because I was so shocked at his disproportionate anger to a routine matter. I felt singled out and persecuted. What a bozo! I was only trying to do my job.

I was still a fairly new Christian at the time, so naturally I recalled one of the few Bible verses that fit the occasion and made me feel good at the time, such as Leviticus 24:19–20:

> If anyone injures his neighbor, as he has done it shall be done to him, fracture for fracture, eye for eye, tooth for tooth; whatever injury he has given a person shall be given to him.

Ooh, that sounded *so good*. It sounded fair, it made sense, and I liked the way it promised injury.

I felt persecuted and wronged. I wanted him to be punished in some way for his gross misconduct and unprofessionalism.

As "punishment" for his behavior, I chose to withhold forgiveness. What an idiotic move on my part. He didn't even notice my cold-shoulder treatment, and he went about the rest of his week as usual while I seethed inside. Needless to say, withholding forgiveness hurt me a whole lot more than it did him.

That weekend, I asked God to open my heart to wholeheartedly extend forgiveness. Each time I remembered the rant, I asked God to remove the sting before it turned to bitterness. It was a prayer I said often that weekend. God graciously granted my request. When that same partner announced he was leaving the firm not long after, I was able to genuinely wish him well. Not only did God unencumber my heart, but He also arranged my circumstances to remove the source of the problem. But it took much prayer and intentionality.

At one time or another, we have all been tempted to withhold forgiveness in order to punish those who hurt us. Let's face it. They had it coming, right? Playing avenger sure feels more gratifying than being the victim.

But when I regressed and started relishing an avenger role, God brought another Bible passage to mind: "If anyone slaps you on the right cheek, turn to him the other also" (Matthew 5:39). Well, *rats!* Time to pray again.

When we feel persecuted or someone has committed an injustice against us, we instantly transition into defensive mode. Such a closed-off position does not lend itself to warm, fuzzy feelings, much less forgiveness.

Jesus promises to provide the strength we need to endure and prevail when we are persecuted. Let's dive into Lesson 6 as we study this "turn the other cheek" edict.

DAY 1:
BIBLICAL
TRUTHS ABOUT
PERSECUTION
AND INJUSTICE

*But I say to you, Love your enemies and pray for those who
persecute you.* (Matthew 5:44)

Jesus taught the Sermon on the Mount, known by some as the Great
Manifesto of the kingdom of God, to His disciples, though multitudes
were present for this teaching. It is arguably the most famous sermon ever
given and contains the longest single teaching given by Jesus in all the
Gospels. For those reasons among others, we lean in to pay close attention.

The latter part of Matthew 5 deals with the relationship of Jesus Christ
to the Law, which lends great insight into the biblical truths regarding
persecution and injustice. When it comes to forgiving those who persecute
us, we need to understand what Jesus taught that day.

Mosaic Law (the laws handed down through Moses) served as the letter
of the Law in Old Testament days. People were expected to follow these
laws or suffer the consequences.

The first five books of the Bible (the Pentateuch) contain specific
regulations designed to set God's people apart from the rest of the world as
God's holy nation. In light of our study, one of God's edicts is particularly
noteworthy.

Write out Exodus 21:23–25.

_____

_____

These verses and others like them provided God's people invaluable
insights into the perfect justice of God's character. When someone hurts us,
this verse tends to comfort us because we know that our hurt contains value
in God's sight.

However, in the Sermon the Mount, Jesus introduces a whole new way for God's people to differentiate themselves from the rest of the world.

Read Matthew 5:38–47. What stands out to you in those passages about God's justice and how He handles persecution?

_____

_____

What radical differences do you notice between the Old Testament teachings regarding persecution and injustice (Exodus 21) and Jesus's teaching (Matthew 5)?

_____

_____

Would Jesus' teaching about proper handling of abuse and injustice be considered radical even today? How do you see that?

_____

_____

We can safely conclude that Jesus is not giving the green light to some thugs to abuse the disciples. So what do you believe Jesus meant when He told them to turn the other cheek when people wounded them?

_____

_____

Some of the most difficult conflicts to sort out consist of those between believers. Being wounded by a fellow brother or sister in Christ can cause more intense pain because we naturally expect a higher standard from another believer.

But the bottom line is that when you and I are hurt, we have a tendency to follow vengeance instead of Jesus. However, Jesus offers specific instructions when a wound is created.

What were His instructions in Matthew 18:15–17?

_____

_____

Sometimes, our offenders refuse to acknowledge their transgressions or to diligently work toward repentance and restitution. But we are not responsible for their actions. We are responsible to obey God's command to forgive. We are to extend forgiveness whether or not they receive or acknowledge it.

I entertained thoughts of how to pay back my boss's unkindness to me. It was exhausting. The more I thought about it, the more I just wanted to forgive him and sleep peacefully again. God is a just God, and He has my back. He has yours, too.

Opportunity for healing begins when we hand persecution and injustice over to God, where it belongs.

Just like Jesus taught.

Pause
for Quiet Reflection

Intentionally schedule at least fifteen minutes of quiet time before the Lord with pen and paper in hand. Ask Him to still your busy mind and open your heart. Take your time reflecting on these questions, and then write down your answers.

1. Have you ever experienced persecution? If so, what was it and how did you process it with God?

_____

_____

2. Scripture never states that you and I are expected to "grin and bear it" or "keep a stiff upper lip" when we are hurt. Have you tried those methods in the past? What was the result?

_____

_____

Apply
It Personally

Now that this lesson has provided some insight from the Word about injustice and persecution, review what you wrote in the Quiet Reflection section above. Spend the next ten minutes in prayer asking God to bring to mind those who have persecuted you or committed injustices against you. Ask God to protect your heart and mind to deflect future attacks. Pray also for Him to begin working in their hearts to turn them toward God instead of further hurtful actions.

God has you in the palm of His hand as you walk through this study individually and together as a group. He promises to bring beauty from ashes, so keep walking.

DAY 2:
LEAVE THE
JUSTICE TO GOD

Let love be genuine. Abhor what is evil; hold fast to what is good. (Romans 12:9)

In our study of forgiveness, a discussion about justice is a must. The pain people inflict on us creates a debt for which restitution must be made. But are you and I the proper ones to carry out justice?

Justice consists of two main components: fairness and consequences. When you are mistreated and respond with this familiar phrase—"It's not fair!"—it indicates that on some level you feel you have been treated unjustly.

The other component deals with consequences. We tend to relish when people get what we think they deserve for their sinful behavior—especially if it was perpetrated against us. It typically sounds like, "Good, she finally got what was coming to her."

But what does the Bible say about fairness and consequences? Write out Leviticus 19:15. Who is responsible for justice in light of forgiving hurt?

_____

_____

What does God say about justice in the following Scripture passages? Psalm 9:7–9

_____

_____

Isaiah 5:16

Romans 3:25–26

Scripture clearly teaches us that justice starts and finishes with God
Himself (see also Psalm 103:9–10; 130:3–4; Acts 17:30–31). God does not
grant us the authority to carry out justice to individuals who hurt us. He
alone reserves that right.

The life of Joseph, which we have been studying, lends great insight
about justice. If you recall, Joseph was sold into slavery by his brothers,
wrongly accused by Potiphar's wife, and thrown into prison, where he spent
many years before being rescued and elevated to power by Pharaoh.

Joseph never attempted to go after justice for the wrongs committed
against him. In fact, Joseph cannot adequately seek justice because how can
justice repay lost time? lost dreams? a lost childhood?

Justice involves setting things right by restoring integrity, wholeness,
and wellness among people and their relationships. And God is all about
relationships.

In Joseph's case, God's justice restored Joseph's integrity by elevating him
to second-in-command over all of Egypt after years of abuse, neglect, and
hardship.

Right and good relationships are at the heart of justice. We find that
justice is closely linked to the word *shalom*, which means "peace," the
absence of conflict and a state of spiritual well-being.

Since God alone has planned our futures, only He fully understands
the justice that needs to be wrought in order to accomplish His plans in our
lives. That is why justice is rightfully left in God's hands.

We may want to see someone who hurt us brought to justice
immediately. And when we say justice, we mean fire, brimstone, and general

mayhem, right? But had God orchestrated immediate justice in Joseph's life, Joseph would have missed out on the crucial life lessons he learned in Potiphar's house and prison, which prepared him for leadership in the most powerful nation on earth at the time.

Take a moment to read Psalms 103 and 130. How do they address justice?

_____

_____

As you read, these psalms beautifully demonstrate that God pursues justice within a context of grace—for both the offender and the one offended.

Forgiving someone does not mean that we have abdicated justice.

We have simply chosen to return justice to where it rightfully belongs: in the hands of our loving, just God.

Shalom.

Pause
for Quiet Reflection

Intentionally schedule at least fifteen minutes of quiet time before the Lord with pen and paper in hand. Ask Him to still your busy mind and open your heart. Take your time reflecting on these questions, and then write down your answers.

1. How would you define or characterize justice in your own words?

_____

_____

2. When you think about your situation, do you believe it is possible to obtain justice apart from God? Why or why not?

_____

_____

Apply
It Personally

Now that this lesson has provided some insight from the Word about forgiveness and justice, review what you wrote in the Quiet Reflection section above. In light of Psalms 103 and 130, spend time in prayer asking God to clarify His role as justice keeper over your life.

God has you in the palm of His hand as you walk through this study individually and together as a group. He promises to bring beauty from ashes, so keep walking.

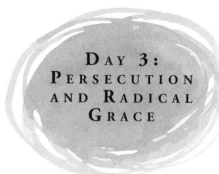

DAY 3:
PERSECUTION
AND RADICAL
GRACE

*But the LORD is with me as a dread warrior; therefore my
persecutors will stumble; they will not overcome me. They
will be greatly shamed, for they will not succeed. Their eternal
dishonor will never be forgotten.* (Jeremiah 20:11)

These days, terrorism is living up to its name: terror. We live in a
world where Christians endure brutal persecution ranging from
loss of opportunity to loss of life. Even in America, less intense forms of
persecution are becoming more prevalent as Christians experience social
marginalization and increased slander.

Such radical persecution naturally demands radical grace. But what does
that have to do with forgiveness? *Everything.*

When you and I are faced with persecution, whether individually or
corporately, we must decide how we will react. Will we run in fear, lash out
in revenge, or face it with faith?

What does Paul tell Timothy in 2 Timothy 3:12?

_____

_____

Did you catch the three-letter word *all*? Paul did not throw in that
word randomly. He relates a vital truth to Timothy: all who confess Christ
as their Savior and publicly live as committed Christians will face various
kinds of persecution during their lifetimes.

Enduring persecution with faith requires us to rely on God and His
Word. In fact, when you and I are not experiencing persecution of some

kind, it begs this question: are we living our faith boldly? Some days, unkind social media exchanges alone answer that question for us.

Jesus Himself encouraged His disciples, knowing they would face terrible persecution. Write out Matthew 5:10:

_____

_____

Blessed when persecuted? Yes. It all comes down to what persecution looks like. At its core, persecution means being reviled, ridiculed, and harassed and enduring false stories told about you. None of this is fun, and all of it can certainly cause much hurt.

Enter forgiveness.

When it comes to responding to those who persecute us, we take a leaf from Paul's teaching. What does he say in 2 Corinthians 12:10?

_____

_____

The first five words provides our motivation: "for the sake of Christ." He loved us so much that He gave His life to redeem. Such unparalleled, matchless love is powerful motivation.

God faithfully and abundantly provides His strength to those facing persecution. He never instructs us to tackle it alone in our human weakness. In our modern world, Christians are martyred every day for their faith.

What does Revelation 6:10–11 say about those martyrs of the faith?

_____

_____

Did you notice that they cried out to the Lord with a loud voice? It is permissible for us to do so, as well. We cannot hide our hurt, frustration, and anger from God. Let it out in the safe space that is God alone. He lovingly absorbs our pain.

In Revelation, white clothing symbolizes the purity of Jesus that now covers the sinner (see also Revelation 3:4–5; 7:9–14; 19:8). Although people who are persecuted are often viewed as being in the wrong, God's Word assures us that facing opposition for our faith is righteous before Him.

When we know God approves of us and has our back, we can draw on faith and persevere in the direst circumstances.

When we experience persecution, God's forgiveness is afforded a wonderful opportunity to shine through us. Various news stories have surfaced over the past year of instances when ISIS terrorists have turned their lives over to Christ because of the radical forgiveness they received from the very Christians they were torturing.

Radical forgiveness can bring about radical change.

Most of us will never receive death threats or be physically tortured because of our faith in Christ Jesus. Nevertheless, as God's precious children, we can rest assured that He will vindicate us when we endure persecution.

What does Revelation 19:1–3 tell us?

You and I can trust that God keeps His promises to the persecuted. How? His Son experienced severe persecution firsthand. Jesus' death on the cross for our sins and His resurrection from the dead prove that God does not abandon the persecuted. God raised His Son and vindicated Him, and God will do the same in His perfect timing for all those who are united to His Son through faith.

As His children, we are persecuted but not abandoned.

Thanks be to God.

Pause
for Quiet Reflection

Intentionally schedule at least fifteen minutes of quiet time before the Lord with pen and paper in hand. Ask Him to still your busy mind and open your heart. Take your time reflecting on these questions, and then write down your answers.

1. **In what ways are you experiencing persecution in this season of your life? If not currently, how have you experienced it in the past?**

_____

_____

2. **Are you finding it difficult to forgive those who are persecuting you? Why or why not?**

_____

_____

Apply
It Personally

Now that this lesson has provided some insight from the Word about the persecution we will endure and forgive, review what you wrote in the Quiet Reflection section above. Spend the next ten minutes in prayer asking God to replace any fear that you have of persecution with a sense of joy that you are enduring it because you are one of His beloved children.

God has you in the palm of His hand as you walk through this study individually and together as a group. He promises to bring beauty from ashes, so keep walking.

Beloved, never avenge yourselves, but leave it to the wrath of God, for it is written, "Vengeance is Mine, I will repay, says the Lord." To the contrary, "if your enemy is hungry, feed him; if he is thirsty, give him something to drink; for by so doing you will heap burning coals on his head." (Romans 12:19–20)

If you have spent any time studying the Old Testament, it should come as no surprise that our God is a God of vengeance. I don't know about you, but I find that description difficult to translate onto Jesus, even though He is part of the Trinity. Jesus is full of grace and truth, mercy, love, and forgiveness. But . . . vengeance?

As we study daring ways to live grace-based forgiveness, vengeance finds no traction here. However, all of us have at one time or another thought about vengeance. Consequently, we need to understand it from a biblical standpoint.

Write out Psalm 94:1.

_____

_____

I must confess that I cringed when I first read this passage. How could our loving Lord be a "God of vengeance"? Some Christians believe God must not be associated with vengeance because we associate vengeance with cruelty and hatred. But since the Bible is God's inspired, inerrant Word, I cannot endorse this belief.

Vengeful people are usually filled with raging, disproportionate anger. The Hebrew word for vengeance in Psalm 94 is *neqamah*. If you read the rest of Psalm 94, you'll see that it discusses stark, violent acts that most of us would rather avoid. It also reveals that God's vengeance does not constitute a senseless surge of divine rage; rather, His vengeance is the exercise of divine justice.

Yet we cannot study God's divine justice without remembering His endless mercy. What do the following passages reveal about God's mercy?

Ephesians 2:4

James 2:13

In His great mercy, God did not dismiss our sins as inconsequential. Rather, He added them to the weight of sin His Son bore on the cross for us, and He remembers them no more.

When we separate God from vengeance and justice, the cross becomes superfluous. And the cross is *anything* but superfluous.

In the following passages, what specific instructions does God give regarding revenge?

Romans 12:19

Deuteronomy 32:35

Most likely, you have experienced hurt and have been tempted to seek revenge. Perhaps you have seen the significant injustice perpetrated throughout our world, and that makes you want to go after the perpetrators with the same measure of atrocities they have dispensed on their victims.

For example, my blood boils when I think of human trafficking and the cruel injustice heaped on those victims. However, Micah 6:8 reminds us that we are to act justly but also to love kindness. In our fallen human nature, desiring vengeance is natural, but we must abdicate that task to God.

As a Houston-area volunteer team leader for Love 146's child anti-trafficking efforts, I find it incredibly difficult to view human traffickers as created and loved by God. Sometimes, it is difficult to sleep at night when a new incident reminds me of the atrocities those traffickers inflict upon children. But we are to *love* and leave the justice to God.

Only in His holy hands will vengeance accomplish the purposes God determines.

Pause
for Quiet Reflection

Intentionally schedule at least fifteen minutes of quiet time before the Lord with pen and paper in hand. Ask Him to still your busy mind and open your heart. Take your time reflecting on these questions, and then write down your answers.

1. **When you're tempted to seek revenge on someone who has hurt you, how do you typically respond?**

_____

_____

2. Upon looking over the verses that talk about God's vengeance, how can we do justice in this world and still be people who love mercy and kindness?

_____

_____

Apply
It Personally

Now that this lesson has provided some insight from the Word about vengeance, review what you wrote in the Quiet Reflection section above. Spend the next ten minutes in prayer asking God to bring to mind those being persecuted in His name. Ask for His protection over them and for His holy vengeance to rescue the victims and restore peace in their lives. And if you are harboring thoughts of revenge or vengeance, ask God to remove those from you and take them on Himself. Remember, specificity is the key.

God has you in the palm of His hand as you walk through this study individually and together as a group. He promises to bring beauty from ashes, so keep walking.

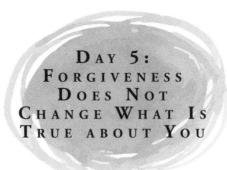

But to all who did receive Him, who believed in His name, He gave the right to become children of God. (John 1:12)

In 1944, General George S. Patton, one of the greatest military commanders in history, delivered a series of speeches to the U.S. Third Army prior to the Allied invasion of Europe. The most famous and well known of his speeches occurred on June 5, 1944, the day before D-day. As the Allied troops geared up to begin the invasion of France, Patton gathered the men and began speaking.

There are many places you can read Patton's actual speech, but I won't quote it here because it's filled with profanity and offensive content. However, if you read past all of that, it becomes clear that Patton issues hardly any commands. He spends the entirety of his speech encouraging his men, telling them what is already true about them: they are equipped, they are brave, they have honor, loved ones are praying for them, and their fellow soldiers will have their backs on the battlefield.

Why is this important for us to know in the context of forgiveness? Because oftentimes when we experience unjust treatment or persecution, we start forming battle plans for retaliation. But before we start garnering troops and drawing lines in the sand, we need to understand what is already true about us.

We learned in Lesson 1 that the word *forgive* in Greek is *aphiēmi*, which means "to send away." Another Greek word that means forgive is *charizomai*, related to the Greek word *charis* (grace). In His grace, mercy, and love, God has already forgiven you. Through your Baptism, He takes your sins and the broken things in you and sends them away.

No one can rob you of your worth in Christ.

When we admit that we cannot fix our own brokenness by drawing up our own battle plans, we are free to abdicate revenge to God and embrace truths about our identity in Christ. We become free to receive His gifts of forgiveness, love, and redemption.

When we are confident of the finished work of Christ in us, we can enter the battlefield of this life extending the gift of forgiveness and waving the flag of peace.

And if such gestures are not reciprocated, God has provided His armor to survive the enemy's attack and emerge victorious on the other side with the shield of faith on our breast and the sword of the Spirit brandishing His truth loud and clear. *Forgiven! Free!*

As we close our lesson, I pray that God abundantly encourages you as you read His Word and learn what He says is already true of you. This is a powerful inventory of your identity in Christ to keep handy and review every now and again. What does God say is true about you in the following verses?

- John 1:12
- John 15:15
- Romans 3:24
- Romans 6:6
- Romans 8:1
- Romans 8:2
- Romans 8:17
- 1 Corinthians 6:19

- 2 Corinthians 5:17
- Galatians 3:28
- Galatians 5:1
- Ephesians 1:4
- Ephesians 1:7
- Ephesians 2:10
- Ephesians 2:13

And there are so many more beautiful truths in the Bible about your identity in Christ. Understanding who you are in Christ makes all the difference. When you understand who you are in Christ, you joyfully embrace what He has called you to do: spread the Gospel to the ends of the earth.

Pause
for Quiet Reflection

Intentionally schedule at least fifteen minutes of quiet time before the Lord with pen and paper in hand. Ask Him to still your busy mind and open your heart. Take your time reflecting on these questions, and then write down your answers.

1. **When was the last time you searched through Scripture to determine who you are in Christ? How did God encourage you?**

2. **How did you feel as you wrote out the verses about your identity in Christ?**

Apply
It Personally

Now that this lesson has provided some insight from the Word about what is already true of you in Christ, review what you wrote in the Quiet Reflection section above. Spend the next ten minutes in prayer asking God to embed in your heart and mind who you are in Him, and thank Him for the privilege of being His beloved child.

God has you in the palm of His hand as you walk through this study individually and together as a group. He promises to bring beauty from ashes, so keep walking.

Small-Group Connection

As a group, take turns discussing some of the things we learned in the homework in Lesson 6.

1. On Day 1, we learned some basic biblical truths about persecution and injustice. Do you find it discouraging that you will face persecution and injustice simply by identifying with Christ? Why or why not?

2. On Day 3, we looked at radical persecution and the radical forgiveness it takes to effect change. When you or a loved one are persecuted for Christ's sake, in what ways do you struggle to forgive?

3. On Day 4, we dove into the sticky topic of God's vengeance and the struggle that some Christians face in labeling God as such. Share your thoughts about our "God of vengeance."

4. We wrapped up this lesson by taking time to list all of the things that are already true about you in your identity with Christ. Which one(s) hit you most profoundly in this season of your life?

Searching the Word Together

Look up and read aloud the following verses. Take turns discussing what strikes you most about forgiving injustice and persecution.

Matthew 18:15–17
Leviticus 19:15
Psalm 9:7–9

Building Deeper Friendships

Understanding that you will face persecution and injustice simply because you identify with Christ can be challenging at times. Pair up with the person sitting across from you and share with each other where you see persecution going on around you or in the world that troubles you. Identify the occurrences, and each of you write down names, places, and circumstances. Switch papers with that person. Carry it with you and pray for those people and circumstances the rest of the week.

Praying as One

Gather back as a group and pray (either have one person pray or several as they feel led) that God will provide you the courage and strength to bravely face persecution and injustice, knowing that our God of vengeance has our back.

Then, ask each person to pray silently for those people who find themselves in various circumstances under persecution.

Going the Extra Mile

Worldwide persecution of Christians is steadily worsening. Work together as a group to identify one or two faith-based organizations that are dedicated to relieving suffering around the world or in your community. Ask someone in the group to research their leadership team and main mailing address. Ask each person in your group to write a short note of encouragement and prayer for the leadership team. Gather all of the notes at your next meeting and mail them to the organization to encourage them in their work in the name of Christ.

FORGIVING YOUR PRODIGALS

Entitled. Self-indulgent. Knucklehead.

Those are just some of the nicer words and names we might call the prodigal son in Luke 15. But I'm not calling him names. They were names I hissed at myself in the mirror in my early 20s.

I grew up in a loving family with parents who cherished my sisters and me. I was never mistreated and rarely went without basic needs met.

But there were tough times when Dad's job hit the slumps. I remember getting ready for my senior prom and having to use a curling iron heated with matches because our electricity had been turned off. I greeted my date in the front yard because I didn't want him knowing that we didn't have money to pay the bills.

And a prodigal daughter was born. Not because I thought I deserved extravagant wealth or even craved it, but money seemed to compensate for a multitude of sins. Consequently, projecting success became my goal. I never again wanted to feel "less than."

But I didn't know Jesus at that stage in my life, and there is no greater "less than," as time would soon reveal.

I landed a good job at a law firm in the tallest building in downtown Houston and was surrounded by successful people with money. So I applied for lots of credit cards and maxed them out trying to fit in. Everything about me looked fine on the outside, but the inside was a wreck about to crumble into a dusty, exhausted heap.

Living the grand life may have been fun to brag about to friends who worked their way through college as waiters, but looking back, I realized that my friends were smarter. They did not live wastefully or recklessly. They lived within their means, took care of their bills, and put money into savings.

It didn't take long for my credit-card debt to become cavernous and the car repo men to began appearing. I could no longer afford my apartment.

Eventually, I swallowed my pride and asked my parents if I could come home. I gave up the lease on my apartment and slinked home with my tail between my legs.

My parents lovingly welcomed me, but I'll never forget the look of pain in their eyes. They wanted to spare me the pain of digging out my self-made mess.

But hardheaded fools have to learn the hard way.

I get the prodigal son because I was a prodigal daughter.

If you've been one, you understand. Maybe you are a parent who has a prodigal child. How can you forgive his or her hurtful, destructive behavior?

The word *prodigal* is the key.

The word *prodigal* means "wasteful." That label certainly fit me. But *prodigal* also means "recklessly extravagant." And that label fits God.

We have a prodigal God. He is our beautiful Creator, who lavishes extravagant love, grace, and mercy on us—the prodigals who wastefully use it, abuse it, and often take it for granted.

When the prodigal son's father welcomed him home, Scripture does not record that the father shook his head, clucked his tongue, or even looked at his son with pain-filled eyes.

Jesus paints a beautiful portrait of a loving father who forgives his child and opens wide his arms. No questions asked.

That's how Jesus welcomes you and me. Every time we seek Him, we find Him waiting with open arms full of grace and love.

Jesus opened wide those same arms on the cross to sacrifice His life for us prodigals. In that singular, mind-blowing act of pure love, He exchanged our sin for the keys to heaven. His blood opened heaven's door to welcome us home eternally.

No matter how far away from God our prodigal feet carry us, our Father never gives up on us.

He never tires of forgiving us.

He never stops scanning the horizon, waiting to run toward us with a royal robe and the family signet ring.

We lay our prodigal heart into His mighty embrace, close our eyes, and find rest in His peace that surpasses all understanding.

And all the while, He strokes our hair, whispering, *"Welcome home, My precious child. Welcome home."*

DAY 1: ENTITLED, SQUANDERING CHILDREN

Not many days later, the younger son gathered all he had and took a journey into a far country, and there he squandered his property in reckless living. (Luke 15:13)

The younger son stared defiantly at his father, disdain dripping from every syllable as he haughtily demanded his inheritance. Immediately.

After all, he had places to go, things to do, and people's affections to buy. Staying home was for losers.

He didn't have time to wait until his father died of natural causes before receiving his inheritance. Instead, the prodigal son basically told his father, "I don't care about you. I care only about your stuff. I wish you were dead."

That's the bottom line as Jesus begins to unfold the parable of the prodigal son in Luke 15.

Although the younger son never articulated those specific words, that's what his words conveyed. *Dad, I wish you were dead.* Despite the insulting audacity of the younger son's request, the father grants it.

Scripture records the father's response as one action: "And he divided his property between them" (Luke 15:12). In Jesus' illustration, the father didn't yell, "How dare you?" or "Get back to work!" He didn't challenge his son, asking, "Just what are you planning to do with what I have spent my life building up?"

He just gives his son what he wants.

Unlike banks and IRAs today, the wealth of a family in those days was tied up in land holdings, homes, and herds. To grant the younger son's self-centered request, the father had to liquidate all he owned and divide the income.

Can you imagine? Total liquidation would have taken time and maneuvering to accomplish, yet Scripture doesn't say the younger son tried to change the process (nor did the older son, I might add). We see no remorse or compassion, only the younger son's greed.

Gimme.

Write out the younger son's words from Luke 15:12.

_____

.

_____

Would you have the nerve to make such a request? In biblical times, parental disrespect was viewed as intolerable. It could have ruined the father's reputation, so it was common to treat such behavior severely. The younger son's father could have literally killed him for such an impertinent request. But the younger son didn't care. He ungratefully demanded what he thought he was entitled to receive.

He was more concerned about spending money than saving relationships.

Entitlement never considers the cost.

What does 1 John 3:17 tell us about entitlement?

_____

_____

At some point, the younger son determined he understood his needs better than his father did, and one day he decided that his self-centered rules needed to take priority.

Although the father gave his younger son what he wanted, the younger son had not lived enough life to understand what he truly needed. I wonder if you and I are any different.

Have you ever looked back at some of the things you asked God to give you and later heaved a huge sigh of relief that He knew better? What were the circumstances?

_____

_____

This parable teaches us the cost of misusing our free will. The further we get from the Father's loving care, the more treacherous our path becomes. Sin inevitably lands us in a far worse state than we were in originally, with the added burden of guilt weighing us down.

Sometimes we have to allow prodigals to be prodigals.

Speaking as a prodigal daughter, experience truly serves as the best teacher. Pain is often the only way to get through the thick skulls of entitled, hardheaded knuckleheads.

God's gift of forgiveness tastes so much sweeter through the haze of self-imposed hardship.

When the father divided the inheritance between his sons, the father gave up part of himself in order to rescue the lost son.

When mankind selfishly grabbed the fruit from the tree in the Garden of Eden, God made the choice in that moment to give up part of Himself. The Father gave up part of the Trinity in order to rescue us.

What does Ephesians 1:11 say regarding inheritance?

_____

_____

Apart from Him, we have no inheritance. Jesus willingly volunteered to give up His share of life in heaven for a time because He knew how much it meant to the Father to be reconciled with His children.

Jesus chose to give His life unto death so we could obtain life.

For our selfishness, we received His selflessness.

The reckless, scandalous love of God is always present in our lives, casting a cross-shaped reminder that He will never leave us or forsake us.

He persistently pursues prodigals to bring us back into relationship with Him.

What a beautiful picture of His lavish forgiveness.

Pause
for Quiet Reflection

Intentionally schedule at least fifteen minutes of quiet time before the Lord with pen and paper in hand. Ask Him to still your busy mind and open your heart. Take your time reflecting on these questions, and then write down your answers.

1. Ask God to reveal where in your life you struggle with prodigal tendencies. It could be money, lust, position, or recognition, to name a few. Name them here and confess them before God.

_____

_____

2. Now that you have named them, ask God to reveal what is the force driving your behavior. Shame? Feeling "less than"? Misplaced priorities? Write your response here.

_____

_____

Applying
It Personally

Now that this lesson has provided some insight from the Word about our prodigal tendencies, review what you wrote in the Quiet Reflection section above. Whether it's shame, self-centeredness, misplaced priorities, or otherwise, ask God to fill that gap with Himself.

Write out the verses below and keep them handy whenever your prodigal tendency raises its head again. I also encourage you to write them on note cards or sticky notes to keep handy around your home or as a bookmark in your Bible.

Philippians 4:19–20

Psalm 68:19

God has you in the palm of His hand as you walk through this study individually and together as a group. He promises to bring beauty from ashes, so keep walking.

D AY 2 :
R E P E N TA N C E :
C O M I N G T O
O U R S E N S E S

Therefore I tell you, whatever you ask in prayer, believe that
you have received it, and it will be yours. (Mark 11:24)

The father's younger son messed up. Big time. After selfishly demanding his inheritance, basically wishing his father dead, and after squandering his inheritance on wild living, the younger son finds himself starving in a pigsty. No money. No food. No prospects.

In Luke 15:17, what conclusion does the younger son reach?

_____

_____

Destitute, with nowhere to turn, the younger son decides to return home. But the son who wants to return is not the same son who left. Life has taught him some hard lessons. In the south, we call it "eating humble pie." The younger son finally understands the collateral damage that his actions caused. *Anguish tends to clarify our perspective.*

What does the son decide to do according to Luke 15:18–19?

_____

_____

Hard-earned experience taught the brash young man that money can buy popularity, but it can't buy friends who will sit with you in a pigsty. *Popularity and poverty don't attend the same parties.*

As soon as the younger son admits that he sinned against his father, we see the signs of repentance.

Repentance is the fuse that ignites forgiveness.

As Christians, you and I hear about repentance on a regular basis. How would you define repentance in your own words?

_____

_____

In the Greek, the word *repentance* paints a word picture of walking in one direction and then turning around and walking in the opposite direction. It's a 180-degree course correction. To repent literally means to "turn away from."

At the beginning of the Ninety-Five Theses, Martin Luther wrote: "When our Lord and Master Jesus Christ said, 'Repent' (Matthew 4:17), He meant that the entire life of believers is to be one of repentance." Luther nailed it. All of life is repentance. It is simply realizing that we mess up, take wrong turns, lose our way in the world's darkness, turn away from that behavior, and eventually ask Jesus to carry us back into the light.

Repentance is an act of strength, not weakness. In repentance, we step out of the shadows, expose our brokenness before God, and receive His restoration with His love.

In the New Testament, the apostle Paul mentions two kinds of repentance. Write out 2 Corinthians 7:9–10.

_____

_____

Paul talks about godly grief and worldly grief (both known as sorrow). You may be wondering why it is important for us to know this. When it comes to forgiveness, we need to recognize these two kinds of repentance to determine whether those who hurt us are offering genuine repentance.

Worldly Sorrow

According to Paul in 2 Corinthians 7:10, to what does worldly sorrow lead?

_____

_____

Worldly sorrow tends to focus on regret over the *consequences* of behavior. It says, "I'm sorry I got caught. I'm sorry I have to face the consequences for what I did." It is a sorrow over the *consequences* we face instead of sorrow over the *hurt* we inflict on others.

Worldly sorrow is self-centered; it focuses on the suffering of "poor little me" as we face the consequences of our actions. It says, "Yes, I did that, but now nobody trusts me anymore. Everybody's talking about me. Everybody's mad at me."

Me is a key word with worldly sorrow. Beware of the person who hurts you and comes to ask forgiveness but continuously focuses on how he or she has suffered.

Worldly sorrow shifts blame and focuses on the consequences.

That's why the Bible says worldly sorrow leads to death. Because as we get older, the severity of our sin changes, and so do the consequences. We see this in children all the time. If you got caught stealing a pencil from a fellow student in elementary school, you received a slap on the hand and had to apologize and give back the pencil. But if you steal a television from a department store in your twenties, you receive a jail sentence and a criminal felony on your record.

Godly Sorrow

Godly sorrow looks much different. According to Paul in 2 Corinthians 7:10, to what does godly sorrow lead?

_____

_____

Godly sorrow says, "I'm sorry for who I've become. I'm sorry that I've become so deceptive and dishonest. I'm sorry for how my behaviors have hurt you and destroyed our relationship." Do you see the difference?

Godly sorrow owns up to the sin and focuses on how to repair the damage, inviting repentance and restitution.

That's why the Bible says godly sorrow leads to salvation and freedom. A person who exhibits godly sorrow determines to walk away from the behavior and move toward repairing the damaged relationship.

Which of these two forms of repentance do you recognize in the younger son?

There have been many times when I have hurt those I love. You probably have too. Read Luke 15. What are the steps toward repentance?

1.

2.

3.

First, we have to acknowledge that we are going in the wrong direction. Luke 15:17 says that the prodigal son "came to himself." This initial stage is usually initiated by a significant amount of pain, hurt, and heartache. The son came to his senses when he hit rock bottom and was looking up from a pigsty, wishing he could eat their slop. We don't choose those moments in life. They happen to us. When they do, they set up the perfect opportunity for the life of repentance.

Second, we have to acknowledge that we have sinned against God and someone else. Luke 15:21 says that the prodigal son proclaimed, "Father, I have sinned against heaven and before you. I am no longer worthy to be called your son." There is an order of importance. First, I sinned against God. Second, I sinned against someone else.

Jesus makes the point in this parable that the prodigal son operated under the false beliefs that his father would not meet his needs and did not understand him. You and I do the very same thing to our heavenly Father when we believe He doesn't come through in the way we think He should.

Before you and I approach someone to repent and ask for forgiveness, that exchange must first happen with our heavenly Father. Why do you think that order is important?

By approaching God first, we acknowledge Him as our Lord and put into action the words of the creed, "I believe in God, the Father Almighty." Thus, we can receive His forgiveness, His cleansing, and the humility to approach those we have hurt. We are strengthened to own up to what we did, admit our fault, ask for forgiveness, and move toward reconciliation (if possible).

Third, we have to formulate a repentance plan. That may sound silly at first, but Jesus provides the prodigal son's example. What is his repentance plan according to Luke 15:18–19?

An effective repentance plan includes the intent to rebuild and make restitution. This is a key step because many people often stop after step 2. They admit they are sorry but do not form a repentance plan to determine how they will rebuild trust and repair the relationship. They simply say, "I'm sorry, that was my bad," and disappear.

Although repentance has been accomplished with steps 1 and 2, reconciliation cannot happen without step 3. Godly repentance always includes all three aspects.

The prodigal son understands that he is no longer worthy to be called a son. *But in God's kingdom, sonship isn't based on worth; it's based on birth.*

When we are born into the kingdom of God through Baptism, we become God's sons and daughters. God has prepared for us a heavenly inheritance because of that birth, not because of our worth. We will never be worthy on our own apart from Christ. His extravagant love paved the way for us to be birthed into an eternal kingdom.

As long as you and I reside on earth, we will hurt one another. Period. So whether we are hurt or we hurt someone else, remember that godly sorrow provides the path toward healing and reconciliation.

Living forgiven.

Living forgiving.

Pause
for Quiet Reflection

Intentionally schedule at least fifteen minutes of quiet time before the Lord with pen and paper in hand. Ask Him to still your busy mind and open your heart. Take your time reflecting on these questions, and then write down your answers.

1. **As you look through the differences between worldly sorrow and godly sorrow, to which do you normally tend to gravitate? Explain.**

2. **If you have hurt someone and repented, did you formulate and execute a repentance plan (step 3)? Why or why not?**

Apply
It Personally

Now that this lesson has provided some insight from the Word about prodigal behavior, review what you wrote in the Quiet Reflection section above. Spend the next ten minutes in prayer asking God to identify any prodigal tendencies in your life, and ask Him to turn you from that road immediately. Remember, specificity is the key.

God has you in the palm of His hand as you walk through this study individually and together as a group. He promises to bring beauty from ashes, so keep walking.

♥

DAY 3:
SCANNING THE HORIZON

But while he was still a long way off, his father saw him and felt compassion. (Luke 15:20)

Yet another day passed. The father shuffled his heavy heart through the daily routine, eyes never leaving the horizon for long. Searching. Scanning. Longing for the return of his prodigal son.

Then one day, dust clouds appear in the distant haze. Puffs kicked up by the rhythm of tired feet. And the father sees his prodigal son come into focus. It's the day he has prayed for since the day his son left.

Wild camels could not keep the father away. What does Luke 15:20 say?

_____

_____

The father runs to his son, covers his tattered clothes with the best robe, puts the family ring on his finger and sandals on his feet, and orders a full-blown celebration.

The son starts his repentance-plan speech, but he never gets to finish it: "Father, I have sinned against heaven and before you. I am no longer worthy to be called your son" (Luke 15:21). The son never even arrives at the part he rehearsed to tell his father that he just wanted to be a hired servant.

The father had already established him as a son.

Galatians 4:1–20 details our sonship in Christ.

Write out Galatians 4:4–7.

_____

_____

We are sons and daughters of God. Once we have reached the bottom of our barrel and feel the embrace of our Father, we can never see ourselves as anything but His child. Every time we sin and run from Him, He wants to welcome us back through His beautiful grace.

It's important to remember that Jesus is relating this parable because He is

- the Son of the Father who would have to forsake His Son for our sake;

- the Son who would not be covered with a robe but stripped naked and humiliated;

- the Son who would be given gall to drink instead of an elaborate feast to enjoy; and

- the Son whose Father will turn away instead of kissing His cheek.

The result of how our heavenly Father will welcome us home is solely and completely because of what Jesus endured for us.

Because of Jesus, your heavenly Father welcomes you with open arms.

He clothes you with His righteousness.

He feeds you with His goodness.

You are His beloved child.

His redeemed prodigal.

His beautiful heir.

What astounding, overwhelming grace He has lavished on you!

Pause
for Quiet Reflection

Intentionally schedule at least fifteen minutes of quiet time before the Lord with pen and paper in hand. Ask Him to still your busy mind and open your heart. Take your time reflecting on these questions, and then write down your answers.

1. Like the prodigal son with his father, when have you felt like you have messed up so badly that you believe forgiveness is impossible? What was the result?

_____

_____

2. Like the prodigal son's father, God never stops searching for us when we stray. Think back on a time when God sought you out and returned you safely home. What were the circumstances and result?

_____

_____

Apply
It Personally

Now that this lesson has provided some insight from the Word about God welcoming us back after we have gone astray, review what you wrote in the Quiet Reflection section above. Spend the next ten minutes in prayer asking God to identify any areas in your life right now where you might be acting like a prodigal child. Ask God to remove those wandering tendencies and draw you back to Himself. Remember, specificity is the key.

God has you in the palm of His hand as you walk through this study individually and together as a group. He promises to bring beauty from ashes, so keep walking.

If we confess our sins, He is faithful and just to forgive us our sins and to cleanse us from all unrighteousness. (1 John 1:9)

Shame is one of the great hindrances we face in receiving God's forgiveness for our prodigal seasons in life. Upon returning to his father's house, it is not far fetched to assume that the prodigal son experienced shame over his behavior. After that prodigal season in my early 20s, I could barely look my parents in the eye when I moved back home. I didn't expect the unconditional love and trust I had received before I initially left home. But I received it in abundance.

To the prodigal son's credit, he does not expect everything to return to normal since he squandered his father's hard-earned money. He just wants to be a servant.

In this parable, Jesus provides a beautiful window through which we glimpse how much God loves humanity. So when the son finally returned, the father who had been watching for him *ran* to his son with compassion, embraced him, and kissed him.

When the son begins reciting his speech, outlining the repentance plan to his father, the father doesn't even let his son get through the whole speech before cutting him off. What happens according to Luke 15:22–23?

_____

_____

Wait! What? Hang on a minute. This kid isn't a military hero returning with a Purple Heart for defending his country. He's a grade-A screw up. *And he knows it.*

Now put yourself in the father's place. If your son had pulled such a stunt and then pulled back into the driveway in his wrecked car, how would you initially react?

_____

_____

My reaction would probably be something like this: "Well, this explanation oughta be good." Or perhaps, "He better be ready to grovel."

But not this father.

And not our heavenly Father.

The reckless, extravagant grace and love of the father eclipses the son's failure. Does God do any less for you and me? Daring, grace-based forgiveness is God's specialty. What do the following verses tell us about God's amazing grace?

2 Corinthians 12:9

_____

_____

Romans 3:23–24

_____

_____

Ephesians 4:7

_____

_____

The prodigal son's father does not simply order some robe to cover his son—he orders the *best* robe. The ring was the family signet ring, a symbol of authority and status. Such a ring was often used to buy and sell goods in biblical times.

Then there's the fattened calf. Only wealthy families owned fattened calves, and they possessed only one. It was specifically set aside for a once-in-a-lifetime celebration to which the whole town would be invited.

We can hardly relate to such a concept in modern times. To lend some perspective, imagine you owned one bottle of wine that was worth thousands and thousands of dollars. It sat for years waiting for that once-in-a-lifetime celebration. What kind of celebration would cause you to uncork and share it?

If it were up to me, a prodigal child returning home after squandering my hard-earned money would probably not cause me to reach for the corkscrew. When observed from a spiritual standpoint, I am thankful God is not so stingy with His love toward me.

As we read the older son's reaction (Luke 15:25–30), one truth becomes crystal clear: *neither son loved the father*. Both sons loved only what their father could give them. They were after the *stuff*, not the relationship.

Such behavior pinpoints the single biggest factor that destroys community: *selfishness*. When we are more interested in someone's possessions instead of their time, that relationship will not endure long.

As if the father's gifts to the prodigal son were not enough, the father orders a celebration to honor his son's return. Write out Luke 15:24

Can you picture the scene? The servants clear the barn. Dad hires a band. Hired hands set up the dance floor. The women roast the prized fattened calf, make potato salad with all the fixings, and order a huge cake from the bakery. Dad sends out invitations over social media. Everyone digs out their party duds and shines their shoes. *This is a big deal.*

Jesus uses this portion of the parable to demonstrate God's reaction when a lost soul repents and returns home. In fact, all three parables in Luke 15 celebrate recovering what had been lost. Read each parable carefully. What had been lost in each of them?

Luke 15:1–7

Luke 15:8–10

Luke 15:11–32

In spite of God's majesty, holiness, universal power, and greatness, He astonishingly cares for individual human beings one at a time.

In Luke 15:1–7, there was one sheep lost out of a hundred. In Luke 15:8–10, there was one coin lost out of ten. In Luke 15:11–32, there was one son lost out of two.

In all three parables, Jesus paints a picture of the God of the universe celebrating a special joy in heaven when one lost sinner repents and returns to Him. It provides a beautiful portrait of how God cares for individuals one at a time.

When it comes to forgiving prodigals, no one does it better than God Himself.

Regardless of how far we stray.

Regardless of the resources we waste along the journey.

Regardless of how much time has passed.

When you and I repent and God turns us back toward Him, the celebration in heaven is epic. So we check shame and guilt at the door and get ourselves out there on that dance floor to join in the celebration.

Let God lead and sweep you off your feet once again.

He has welcomed you home.

Pause
for Quiet Reflection

Intentionally schedule at least fifteen minutes of quiet time before the Lord with pen and paper in hand. Ask Him to still your busy mind and open your heart. Take your time reflecting on these questions, and then write down your answers.

1. **If you have gone astray along your faith walk, how did God turn you back toward Himself? If not you, then how have you witnessed that in someone else's faith walk?**

2. **How did God use that season in your life to grow your faith? Where did that growth show itself most clearly?**

Apply
It Personally

Now that this lesson has provided some insight from the Word about God searching for us and welcoming us after we have gone astray, review what you wrote in the Quiet Reflection section above. Spend the next ten minutes in prayer thanking God for the incredible gift of faith that He has given to you. Thank God for His tenacious love to search for you no matter how far you ran yesterday or today or will run tomorrow.

God has you in the palm of His hand as you walk through this study individually and together as a group. He promises to bring beauty from ashes, so keep walking.

And he said to him, "Son, you are always with me, and all
that is mine is yours." (Luke 15:31)

The tax collectors and sinners drew near to listen. The Pharisees and scribes drew near to grumble. It was a typical day in the life of Jesus. Luke 15 opens with Jesus settling down to tell three parables about what it means to be lost and then found.

The sinners and tax collectors (those bottom-of-the-barrel people, according to religious leaders) were welcome company to Jesus. The Pharisees (outwardly good, churchgoing folks) chose once again to show their hypocrisy in high-definition color by grumbling. I find it interesting that the very people Jesus chose to love were not loved by those who purportedly loved God most.

What do the Pharisees specifically grumble about in Luke 15:2?

_____

_____

Personally, I am thankful Jesus received sinners and ate with them. These two groups of people bear discussing. When Jesus encountered people in the Gospels, they usually fell into one of two camps: (1) those who had taken wrong turns in life but found love, grace, and acceptance in Jesus, and (2) the religious folks who had always done the outwardly proper thing yet their hearts were far from God.

When Jesus begins the third parable, He starts teaching about a prodigal son. But within that story, we are introduced to the prodigal son's older brother. The brothers fit perfectly into the two camps to whom Jesus is teaching. The prodigal son was a sinner drawing near. The older son was outwardly good but inwardly grumbling.

Grumbling never stays inward for too long.

In the previous lesson, we looked at the prodigal son. For this lesson, we are turning our attention to the older son.

In context of the older son's portion of this parable, Jesus emphasizes a concept called "spiritual lostness." You and I can be spiritually lost by being bad (the younger son) or by being good (the older son). Why lost? Because neither son initially relied on the grace, mercy, and forgiveness of God.

Each had his own salvation plan.

The older son first appears in the parable in Luke 15:25. Write that verse here.

_____

_____

Nothing seems wrong, right? Now write out Luke 15:28–29.

_____

_____

What happened between verses 25 and 29 that caused the older son's attitude to change?

_____

_____

This part of the parable is uncomfortable. I wonder if the Pharisees in Jesus' crowd realized some similarities. It is difficult to look at the older son because "good" church people sometimes act similarly. These people have done all the right exterior works. But what about their hearts? The good don't consider that they are lost. Physically, they are present. But once again, what about their hearts?

Younger-son-lostness ends up in the pigsties of the world. But older-son-lostness usually ends up in church. The younger son eventually repents, returns home, and is restored. But the older son is already home doing what is expected of any "good" son.

When the father invites the older son to celebrate the return of his wayward brother, the older son refuses to join the party. Consequently, the older son is lost. He turns down fellowship with his father, his brother, and his community.

Some may argue that maybe the older son eventually accepted the invitation, but we know he doesn't because these are fictional characters. They are being used by Jesus to illustrate a point, and they have no life outside of the story. Because of unforgiveness, the older son remains lost.

That's the whole point.

The one who was lost because of his badness actually finds his place in the kingdom of God, but the one lost in his own goodness is really lost.

There are several points in the parable that help us identify if we suffer from older-brother-lostness.

Older brothers live with an undercurrent of anger. When the older brother heard about the party for the younger son, he became angry. The significance of the father's gifts to the prodigal son added fuel to the older son's bitter reaction and resentment. Take a minute to paraphrase the older son's reaction from Luke 15:25–28.

Older brothers claim they always follow the rules and never disobey their fathers. They harbor resentment because they believe they've done their share and are always in the right. However, they have a skewed view of their own level of obedience. They say. "I've *never* disobeyed," but only because they do not classify the bad things they do as sin; only *other people* commit sins. Older brothers are highly critical and can find something wrong with everything. Have you ever known some church people like that? Are you an older brother?

Older brothers believe they are entitled. Older brothers walk around with a sense of entitlement that says, "God, You owe this to me because I've been so good and never messed up."

How do you see this in Luke 15:29?

_____

_____

How do you see this in your own life?

_____

_____

Older brothers believe God owes them for how hard they've worked and for their unwavering obedience, so they expect God's blessings. They find God useful because as long as they do what they're supposed to do, then God should be blessing them. When they don't receive those blessings, they get angry.

Older brothers live with an oppressive sense of obligation. Everything the older brother does for God is a "grind" because it's not done out of love and affection, but out of a sense of duty. They typically say, "We're all supposed to do it, but I'm the only one who follows the rules!" Older brothers serve, pray, study Scripture, and tithe like good religious people are supposed to do, but they find no joy in any of it.

They pray regularly because they think as long as they're telling God what they've done and what they need, _then_ God should give them what they want. But if God doesn't answer them in the right time or the right way, then the anger and grumbling kick in. Their religion is merely another obligation, so they become bitter. They turn these actions into law instead of a loving response to God's grace and mercy.

How do you see this in Luke 15:30?

_____

_____

Did you take note of the older brother's words? *"When this son of yours . . ."* The older brother doesn't even call him his brother! He distances himself from his younger brother because of his younger brother's behavior. That's the superior, judgmental, moral attitude older brothers have. They look down on those who are not like them—uncouth, not religious enough, not educated enough, or not rich enough. They are the ones in church who look down on people not dressed like they "should be" rather than rejoicing in the fact that those people are even in church at all.

What does Romans 2:1–2 say about such an attitude?

_____

_____

When the younger son messes up, he believes he has lost the right be to a son, so he asks to be a servant. The older son remains obedient, yet he sees himself as a servant, even though he is a son.

Rarely in the life of an older son do we see a sense of adoration for God. We see lots of requests and propriety, but not a lot of loving God for how wonderful and beautiful He is.

Jesus gave only one command in all four Gospels, and He says the same thing four different times: *"Love one another as I have loved you."* Write out two of these occurrences below.

John 15:12–13

_____

_____

Matthew 22:37–39

_____

_____

Jesus could easily look at our lives with an older-brother mentality. But He doesn't. He reaches out in love and grace to all. Older brothers reach out only to those whom they determine are deserving or worthy of their goodness.

The truth is that we can all be older brothers. No matter how much we try to be humble before God, we think that since we're *inside* church, we are a little better than those *outside* of it. Or worse, we glance down the church pew and determine we are better than "those people over there." As though somehow we deserve God's love, blessings, and grace more than *those* people.

The younger son reached the bottom and saw no other options. But older brothers rarely see their lostness. They fail to realize how their self-righteous, overcritical, and dutiful lifestyles are sucking the very love of Jesus Christ out of their hearts.

Who are you in this story? Whether you identify as the prodigal son or older son, the father's response to his older son is God's response to us.

Write out Luke 15:31.

Like he did with the younger son, the father extends forgiveness and grace to the older son. The Greek word for son here is *teknon*, which means "child." This is a beautiful illustration of how God chases older sons with love—just as He chases younger sons.

Through the father, God conveys that there's nothing you can do that could make Him love you more than He already does. Or any less.

According to Jeremiah 31:3, how does God love you?

Whether you are doing all the right things or you are messing up, you belong to God.

Pause
for Quiet Reflection

Intentionally schedule at least fifteen minutes of quiet time before the Lord with pen and paper in hand. Ask Him to still your busy mind and open your heart. Take your time reflecting on these questions, and then write down your answers.

1. After working through this lesson, in what way(s) do you identify yourself as the older son? the younger son?

2. If you identify as an older son, which of the attributes above do you struggle with the most? Anger? Entitlement? Oppressive obligation?

3. If you identify as a younger son, which of the attributes do you struggle with? Selfishness? Taking the Father's love for granted? Squandering?

Apply
It Personally

Now that this lesson has provided some insight from the Word about the unforgiving sibling, review what you wrote in the Quiet Reflection section above. Spend the next ten minutes in prayer asking God to clarify which son you resemble. Ask God to reveal to you the behaviors that need to be changed and expanded upon for the good of His kingdom. Remember, specificity is the key.

God has you in the palm of His hand as you walk through this study individually and together as a group. He promises to bring beauty from ashes, so keep walking.

♥

Small-Group Connection

As a group, take turns discussing some of the things we learned in the homework in Lesson 7.

1. On Day 1, we dug into the entitled, squandering younger son. Can you relate to his choices and behaviors? If you feel comfortable, share your experiential wisdom with the group.

2. Repentance literally means coming to our senses and turning around to go the opposite way. Have you ever experienced that crossroads? What circumstance brought you back to your senses?

3. On Day 3, we see the beautiful picture of the prodigal son's father scanning the horizon to watch for his son's return. What peace and comfort do you find knowing that God does that for you when you go astray?

4. We wrapped up this lesson by comparing how both sons responded to their father. Which traits of which son best identifies you during this time in your life?

Searching the Word Together

Look up and read aloud the following verses. Take turns discussing what strikes you most about each regarding our forgiving God.

Luke 15:22–24
Luke 15:31–32

Building Deeper Friendships

God extends forgiveness to both the younger son and the older son. The younger son had been humbled by circumstances and leaped at the father's invitation to restore him. The older son relied on his keeping of the rules to maintain an untarnished reputation and declined the father's invitation. If possible, pair up with someone you have not yet paired up with and share which son you most identify with during this season of life and why.

Praying as One

Gather back as a group to pray (either have one person pray or several as they feel led) and offer God thanks, because regardless of which son you identify with, God extends forgiveness and restoration to all who repent and genuinely seek Him for it.

Then in a moment of silence, ask each person to pray silently for the person they paired up with to share their story.

Going the Extra Mile

It is important for every Christian to understand how God longs for an intimate relationship with His children. We are not a faceless herd to Him. He sees each one of us, our challenges, our joys, and our heartbreaks. Take time this next week to write out Psalm 139 once each day. Whether first thing in the morning, during your lunch break, or before you go to bed, pull out your Bible and a notepad and write out all of Psalm 139 once a day for seven days. This psalm reaffirms how much God loves you from the moment He thought of you before the foundation of the world.

Especially on those hard days you experience, you need to be reminded just how much you are loved by the One who created you.

Lesson 8

FORGIVING LIKE JESUS, OUR GOOD SHEPHERD

Sheep are not very bright. Driven by their appetite, they walk with their heads down to scope out the next grazing spot. They've even been known to walk off cliffs while grazing because they don't pay attention to their surroundings.

Frankly, that sounds like me. Driven by all kinds of appetites, whether success, social status, or some other craving, many days I find my head buried in my own agenda. Some days I wonder if I actually maintained eye contact in a conversation with another human being longer than five seconds.

Thankfully, our Good Shepherd knows how to handle sheep like you and me.

We are prone to wander in search of something we think we are missing, whether it is worldly excitement, adventure, or the latest technological gadget. Or perhaps we feel entitled to something that God has not given us, such as a job, a spouse, or a family.

But there's one fascinating aspect about sheep where we differ greatly. Sheep are vulnerable. They have no natural defense mechanisms. They know only to stomp their feet when predators approach. Not very effective, right?

You and I can certainly be vulnerable, but we have an effective defense mechanism: our mouths. Sticks and stones can break our bones, but words have the potential to destroy us. When we are hurt or angry, our words can cause catastrophic damage in another person's life. When I think back at some of the ugly things I have said to loved ones over the years, I just want to crawl into a hole.

Our words are one of the main reasons forgiveness is critically necessary. Although actions can certainly cause harm, words are often our weapon of choice.

When we read through the Gospels, we see that Jesus used His words to build up people, to speak the truth in love, and to forgive sins.

Jesus demonstrated that forgiveness is not a solitary, momentous act but an intentional, repetitive lifestyle.

Forgiveness requires us to let go of a debt, then another, and yet another. It necessitates facing our pasts to relive hurtful moments and then to surrender them at the foot of the cross.

One final note about sheep. They are naturally dirty creatures. They never clean themselves. Likewise, you and I are born dirty with sin. *(Thank you, Adam and Eve.)* We can clean our exterior, but no amount of scrubbing can remove our sinful nature.

A stain is a stain. Filth is filth.

Yet God continues to pursue you with matchless love. He guides you. He knows your name. I pray you know His voice. He provides for your every need.

And He protects you, so you can confidently say, "I will fear no evil" (Psalm 23:4).

As we wrap up our study, we saved the best stories for last: the ones about Jesus Himself. Let's dig into these stories where our Good Shepherd moved in close to personally forgive a few weary souls who did not believe they deserved it.

Perhaps that's you today.

Lean in and hear Jesus' words of forgiveness *for you.*

Be kind to one another, tenderhearted, forgiving one another,
as God in Christ forgave you. (Ephesians 4:32)

When Jesus taught His followers how to pray, He told them, "Forgive us our debts, as we also have forgiven our debtors" (Matthew 6:12). He intentionally connected the forgiveness we receive with the forgiveness we are to offer.

Jesus' words conveyed with unmistakable clarity that we are to allow the gift of forgiveness given *to* us to flow *through* us to those around us.

As I began writing this book, one friend asked, "I hear about forgiveness all the time and know what it means, but exactly how am I supposed to *teach* it?" What a great question!

First of all, the most effective method we can use to teach a lifestyle of forgiveness is modeling it. We have looked at several Bible stories that show how to receive and extend forgiveness, but there are three stories that rise above the others when it comes to teaching forgiveness principles to others.

1. Jesus from the Cross

And when they came to the place that is called The Skull, there they crucified Him, and the criminals, one on His right and one on His left. And Jesus said, "Father, forgive them, for they know not what they do." And they cast lots to divide His garments. . . . Then Jesus, calling out with a loud voice, said, "Father, into Your hands I commit My spirit!" And having said this He breathed His last. (Luke 23:33–34, 46)

The first aspect of forgiveness that needs to be understood and taught is that Jesus is the only reason we receive and extend forgiveness. We all make mistakes, and because of Jesus, we are forgiven.

The story of Jesus dying on the cross not only teaches forgiveness but also shares the Gospel. Even if you have previously shared the Gospel, knowing that nothing the hearers do, say, or think separates them from the love of Jesus can ever be heard often enough.

Write out Romans 8:38–39 here.

_____

_____

Specifically teach that when we approach Jesus and admit our need for His forgiveness, He always responds to us with open arms. It is precisely because of Jesus' example that we know how to respond to others.

What does 1 John 4:19 tell us?

_____

_____

We love (and forgive) because He first loved (and forgave) us.

2. The Prodigal Son

I will arise and go to my father, and I will say to him, "Father, I have sinned against heaven and before you. I am no longer worthy to be called your son. Treat me as one of your hired servants." And he arose and came to his father. But while he was still a long way off, his father saw him and felt compassion, and ran and embraced him and kissed him. And the son said to him, "Father, I have sinned against heaven and before you. I am no longer worthy to be called your son." But the father said to his servants, "Bring quickly the best robe, and put it on him, and put a ring on his hand, and shoes on his feet. And bring the fattened calf and kill it, and let us eat and celebrate. For this my son was dead, and is alive again; he was lost, and is found." And they began to celebrate. (Luke 15:18–24)

As a beloved child in God's family, we are all forgiven and welcome—regardless of how bad we mess up. In Luke 15, the father's younger son rudely demands his inheritance, leaves home, and then squanders it all. The money runs out, and the son is in a desperate situation of his own making. When he comes to his senses, he prepares a repentance speech and turns back toward home. He plans on asking his father if he can return as a hired servant. Instead, his father welcomes him home as a son.

This story emphasizes perfectly how we are a part of God's family—His precious children. Write out the following verses that clarify our place in God's family.

1 John 3:1

_____

_____

Romans 8:16

_____

_____

Galatians 3:26

_____

_____

No matter how far we wander, God loves us and forgives us. But it is important to emphasize that God's forgiveness is not a free pass to sin recklessly. It is precisely His love and forgiveness that provide great motivation to choose what is right in every situation.

When we make bad choices, we are still part of God's family. Like parents who do not leave their children just because they mess up, God does not abandon us when we mess up. When we realize our mistakes, turn away from them, and ask for forgiveness, He is always ready to love us and welcome us home.

3. Parable of the Unforgiving Servant

> Then Peter came up and said to Him, "Lord, how often will my brother sin against me, and I forgive him? As many as seven times?" Jesus said to him, "I do not say to you seven times, but seventy-seven times." (Matthew 18:21–22)

Just as Jesus forgives us, He instructs us to forgive others time and time again. Here, we see Him clearly teaching His disciples they are to forgive over and over—"seventy-seven times." The point is not that we are to keep count and when they reach the limit, the relationship is over. Jesus makes the point that His forgiveness never runs out, and neither should ours.

Only Jesus provides the motivation and true model for humility and forgiveness. Why do you believe that is important?

_____

_____

In this fallen world, parents, siblings, teachers, friends, and loved ones will make mistakes that hurt us. It is vital to teach that the mistakes we make affect others, so it is important to humbly ask for forgiveness (Ephesians 4:32).

We are not responsible for someone else's willingness to receive our forgiveness (or God's), but we can be at peace knowing we followed Jesus' command and example to extend it wholeheartedly.

Pause
for Quiet Reflection

Intentionally schedule at least fifteen minutes of quiet time before the Lord with pen and paper in hand. Ask Him to still your busy mind and open your heart. Take your time reflecting on these questions, and then write down your answers.

1. **Are you intentional about learning to receive and extend forgiveness? If so, how? If not, why?**

_____

_____

2. **If you teach people in some capacity, how do you intentionally teach them biblical forgiveness principles?**

_____

_____

Apply
It Personally

Now that this lesson has provided some insight from the Word about modeling and teaching forgiveness, review what you wrote in the Quiet Reflection section above.

Think about your week. If someone hurt you, whether a lot or a little, consider humbly approaching them the next time you see them to let them know their words or actions hurt you and how they affected you. Give them a chance to make things right.

God has you in the palm of His hand as you walk through this study individually and together as a group. He promises to bring beauty from ashes, so keep walking.

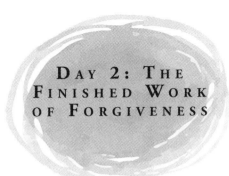

DAY 2: THE FINISHED WORK OF FORGIVENESS

In Him we have redemption through His blood,
the forgiveness of our trespasses, according to the riches
of His grace. (Ephesians 1:7)

A few years ago on a chilly May morning, I walked into the Palace of Holyroodhouse in Edinburgh, Scotland. As I stood in Mary, Queen of Scots's bedchamber, my gaze was instantly riveted on an extraordinary picture hanging on a wall. It was an oil on canvas painting called "The Adoration of the Kings," created by artist Andrea Schiavone (ca. 1510–1563).

The beautiful artwork depicts a seated Virgin Mary, holding Jesus, with Joseph standing behind her as though asleep. Three kings have come to offer their gifts to the newborn King. The Christ Child leans forward toward the gifts, eager to receive them. In the background, an ox peeks in from the edge. Two doves perch on the shadowed stable roof. A boy holding a billowing flag sits on a horse.

The painstaking detail reflected on every square inch is truly exceptional. There is no room to add anything else to the masterpiece—it is a completed work.

It is a finished work, preserved over the centuries.

We cannot contribute to a finished work. We cannot complete a completed work. That is the point of Jesus' sacrifice to forgive our sins. Our sins are all forgiven. Our salvation is won. A finished work by Christ, completed on Calvary. We cannot add a single thing to it.

Forgiven. The word is written on our foreheads and etched across our hearts. It's a genuine, true, and finished work. I may not always *feel* worthy of His forgiveness, but that doesn't change the fact of it.

Write out 1 John 2:12.

_____

_____

It is not by our works that our sins are forgiven, but *on account of His name.* It is His finished work, preserved for us since before the foundation of the world.

Why do you believe it is important to know that our forgiveness is a finished work?

_____

_____

It is vital for us to understand that it is not our works that bring us blessings—it is Christ's finished work. Living out a vibrant Christian life is not about working to earn His forgiveness, but believing in the completed work He has already accomplished. Jesus leans in to receive what we offer Him (like the painting's Christ Child), but our forgiveness is not based on what we offer. Like Peter on that beach in John 21, we are forgiven and restored based solely on what Christ has already achieved on our behalf.

It is important to note that although we offer Christ our service, works, adoration, worship, and love, there is nothing we can offer Him that makes us more acceptable or more loved. Although He accepts these things we offer, His acceptance does not equate salvation. That beautiful work was secured by Christ alone on the cross of Calvary.

Because Christ's work is finished, of what does Isaiah 53:5 remind us?

_____

_____

His sacrifice healed us from the inside out. The victory is won. You may be faced with overwhelming difficulties today, but the ultimate victory is already won.

What did Jesus proclaim in John 19:30?

_____

_____

Jesus forgives all of our past, present, and future sins. Some people who become Christians as adults operate under the misconception that God forgave all our past sins up until that point, but that future sins are not forgiven until we confess them and ask God's forgiveness. Been there, done that.

When Jesus died on the cross, *all* of our sins were future sins. There is no sin we commit that He cannot, did not, or has not already forgiven on Calvary.

All of them. Your confession does not cleanse you from your sins; only the blood of Jesus cleanses you. Jesus took on the weight of all of your sins and made an atonement to God for all.

Write out Ephesians 1:7.

_____

_____

Baptism, or God's Word connected to the water, is God's action to bestow on us the gift of faith. Through this gift of faith, God initiates our relationship with Him.

When we receive the Lord's Supper, God gives us the true body and blood of Christ for the forgiveness of our sins. Before we approach the Lord's Table and each day of our life, a key part of our faith life is confession. When we confess our sins to God, we receive His absolution for them. However, confession does not *earn* God's forgiveness; it was secured on the cross by Christ Himself.

What does 2 Corinthians 5:21 say about Jesus' work on the cross regarding our sin?

_____

_____

When Jesus hung on the cross, He became sin—for us. God poured out His just wrath on Christ as a ransom for sin. Christ alone won the peace between God and man. Christ alone completed the work of reconciling us to God. Christ takes the burden of our sin and gives in exchange His complete forgiveness and love.

We cannot add works or brushstrokes to Jesus's masterpiece, painted by His blood more than two thousand years ago. In that moment, He paid our debts in full. He preserved an eternal future with Him for all who believe by faith that Jesus lived, died, and rose again to forgive our sins.

A *finished* work.

There is no more beautiful masterpiece.

Triumphant grace!

Pause
for Quiet Reflection

Intentionally schedule at least fifteen minutes of quiet time before the Lord with pen and paper in hand. Ask Him to still your busy mind and open your heart. Take your time reflecting on these questions, and then write down your answers.

1. **As we looked at Christ's finished work of forgiveness, what hope or assurance does that bring to you today?**

2. **Reread Ephesians 1:7 and Isaiah 53:5. What comfort do His promises bring to you today?**

Now that this lesson has provided some insight from the Word about the finished work of Christ, review what you wrote in the Quiet Reflection section above.

If you were to paint a picture of forgiveness, what would it look like? Mine would simply be a white canvas with one red line meandering through it. Our sins have been washed white as snow by the blood of Christ. Thank You, Lord.

God has you in the palm of His hand as you walk through this study individually and together as a group. He promises to bring beauty from ashes, so keep walking.

DAY 3:
FORGIVEN OUTCASTS

*In Him we have redemption through His blood, the
forgiveness of our trespasses, according to the riches of His
grace, which He lavished upon us.* (Ephesians 1:7–8)

Scripture does not give us her name, age, or background. But we know
one thing for certain: she sold physical affection for monetary gain. Her
shameful lifestyle was well known among the people. Everyone whispered,
avoided eye contact, and shunned her presence. *Especially* the religious
people.

Everyone except Jesus.

One day Jesus accepted a dinner invitation in her town. Here's how the
story goes:

> One of the Pharisees asked Him to eat with him, and He went
> into the Pharisee's house and reclined at table. And behold,
> a woman of the city, who was a sinner, when she learned that
> He was reclining at table in the Pharisee's house, brought an
> alabaster flask of ointment, and standing behind Him at His
> feet, weeping, she began to wet His feet with her tears and
> wiped them with the hair of her head and kissed His feet and
> anointed them with the ointment. (Luke 7:36–38)

This event was a large public dinner at Simon's house. The Pharisees
placed high importance on how people perceived them. So let's say this

happened at your house and you are a Pharisee. How would you have reacted?

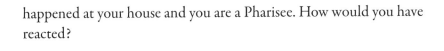

In the custom of that time, Jesus would have reclined at a low table, propping Himself up on His left elbow, eating with His right hand. Then this woman appeared, uninvited and with unacceptable credentials (according to the Pharisees). Various versions of Scripture refer to her as an especially wicked sinner and an immoral woman. Let's face it, a detailed list of her sins wasn't necessary because the world's oldest profession has hardly changed over the millennia.

She stumbled in alone carrying a small alabaster flask of perfume. The most expensive, precious item she owned was also the currency of her profession.

Perhaps she merely wanted to see Jesus. To lay eyes on the One she heard people talk about. This man who was *different*. We don't know if she merely intended to anoint His head, a common gesture of respect. We know only what Scripture records.

She wept.

So profuse and prolonged was her weeping that she was able to wash Jesus' feet with her tears and dry them with her hair. It's that anguished crying that pours out sorrow from a hurting soul.

She never said a word. She didn't have to. *Every word her actions uttered was heard by all.* She sank to her knees and then bowed her head so low it touched the ground.

Jesus didn't draw back, reprimand her, or call her names. He silently received the gift of her tears, recognizing her heartfelt actions for what they were—worship.

But she wasn't finished. She pulled out her alabaster flask and poured that costly perfume on His feet—almost as if she was pouring away her old life in hopes of receiving a new one. It was the same perfume she wore to lure customers. The smell alone confirmed her profession.

The exchange was silent. The effect was profound. *The meaning was significant.*

Well, Simon the Pharisee had had enough. What is his response in Luke 15:39?

_____

_____

Did you notice that Simon did not voice his comment aloud? Just a word to the wise: Jesus knows all things spoken and unspoken, so watch what you *think*.

Jesus then launches into what initially seems like a random tale: "A certain moneylender had two debtors. One owed five hundred denarii, and the other fifty. When they could not pay, he cancelled the debt of both. Now which of them will love more?" (Luke 7:41–42).

Naturally, Simon the Pharisee had no choice but to answer, "The one, I suppose, for whom he cancelled the larger debt" (Luke 7:43). Jesus gives him kudos for the right answer and then proceeds to delineate all the ways Simon had slighted Jesus since His arrival (Luke 7:44–46). He basically told Simon he had the hospitality skills of a death-row guard.

What question does Jesus ask Simon in Luke 7:44?

_____

_____

Up to that point, Simon had not verbally acknowledged the presence of the woman. However, Jesus did not want Simon to lose sight of the point or the woman. Simon saw a prostitute, not a person. But not Jesus. He welcomed her touch. He met her gaze. And by doing so, He acknowledged her value as God's image bearer.

What does Jesus tell Simon in Luke 7:47?

_____

_____

He called her forgiven. This woman's tears, her hair, her kisses, and her perfume poured out *love* over Jesus' feet.

The lesson for us about the Shepherd's forgiveness is contained in His words to Simon: "He who is forgiven little, loves little" (Luke 7:47). If you and I truly understood the totality of the great many sins God has forgiven us, we would be reduced to tears of gratitude as well.

Jesus told the woman, and He tells us, "Your sins are forgiven" (Luke 7:48). Not *perhaps*, not *maybe,* not *if.* But *done.* Thank You, Jesus.

According to Luke 7:50, what is the result of His forgiveness?

_____

_____

Who doesn't need more peace in life? Jesus is the Lord of peace. In fact, "the God of peace" is a title used numerous times in Scripture. Look up and write out a few examples in following verses.

Romans 15:33

_____

_____

Philippians 4:9

_____

_____

Hebrews 13:20

_____

_____

God's forgiveness in Christ Jesus brings peace that "passes all understanding." What were Jesus' parting words to the woman in Luke 7:50?

_____

_____

I pray that we, like this woman, *demonstrate* our love for a God who forgives completely—regardless of who is watching or how uncomfortable the situation may be.

Pause
for Quiet Reflection

Intentionally schedule at least fifteen minutes of quiet time before the Lord with pen and paper in hand. Ask Him to still your busy mind and open your heart. Take your time reflecting on these questions, and then write down your answers.

1. **How can you know, as surely as this woman did, that your sins are forgiven?**

_____

_____

2. **Look up and write out Romans 4:7 and Romans 5:8. What comfort do these promises bring to you today?**

_____

_____

Apply
It Personally

Now that this lesson has provided some insight from the Word about the Shepherd's forgiveness, review what you wrote in the Quiet Reflection section above.

Sometime today, stand in front of the mirror and look yourself in the eye. Say out loud, "God forgives you!" Say it again. And again. Confess to God, repent of your transgressions, and receive His promised forgiveness for your sins, both known and unknown, through His body and blood.

We may see ourselves as very different from the sinful woman. But we aren't, are we? We are all among the *forgiven much*, covered in His love, drenched in His grace. Thank You, Jesus.

God has you in the palm of His hand as you walk through this study individually and together as a group. He promises to bring beauty from ashes, so keep walking.

DAY 4: "DO YOU LOVE ME?"

And after saying this He said to him, "Follow Me." (John 21:19)

Have you ever done something so terrible, so unthinkable, that you believed you did not *deserve* God's forgiveness?

Peter thought he had.

After swearing to Jesus that he alone would never leave Jesus, Peter swore he didn't even *know* Him. Not that he had not *seen* Jesus lately, but emphatically, "Man, I do not *know* what you are talking about" (Luke 22:60).

Then as the rooster crow signaled his failure, Peter locked eyes with Jesus across that dark courtyard. It's bad enough turning your back on a friend in need. But to declare you never will and then end up doing it? And not just a friend, but your Savior?

Then Jesus was crucified, died, and was buried.

Peter thought it was all over. He failed, and he couldn't make it right. Jesus was gone. So he did something we all do when we lose hope: *he sought comfort in the familiar.*

Even after walking with Jesus for three years and seeing countless miracles, signs, and wonders, Peter decided to return to what he knew best: *fishing.*

Think of what hangs in the balance during that time. Jesus has been resurrected and is about to ascend into heaven to take His place at God's right hand for all eternity. It's one of the most critical times in all of history.

Yet Peter and the disciples are in confusion. They don't know what they are supposed to do next, so what does Peter do? He returns to what's familiar. He goes fishing.

Have you ever, in the most critical time of your leadership or ministry, when everything's on the line and everything seems to be coming together, been so aware of your weaknesses and shortcomings that you simply wanted to go back to what's familiar?

That's exactly what Peter decides to do. And sometimes, we follow suit.

Instead of reengaging with Jesus and receiving His promised forgiveness, we choose to go fishing. I don't mean literally. I mean physically, emotionally, and spiritually, we go back to the one thing we know best: the easiest path.

The scary thing about when confused Christians go fishing is that we often take others with us. Just like Peter did. He climbed in the boat to escape, and the others went with him.

There's an unspoken test here for us: when the quorum goes fishing, do we automatically join?

But Jesus would not let His disciples remain checked out. Read John 21:1–7. What question does Jesus ask in John 21:5?

_____

_____

Did you notice He calls them *children?* That's a relationship term. In that one word, Jesus conveys His willingness to repair the damage. He knew they were stumbling backward in failure and were ashamed, but He still wanted them. In His perfect love and endless forgiveness, Jesus still wants to show us His saving grace and love us.

Has running away mentally or physically ever worked for anybody? Has it solved anything long term? We have to assure those who are running of who they are in light of the sheer grace, love, and perfect forgiveness of God: *His children.*

> Jesus said to them, "Children, do you have any fish?" They answered Him, "No." He said to them, "Cast the net on the right side of the boat, and you will find some." So they cast it, and now they were not able to haul it in, because of the quantity of fish. (John 21:5–7)

The disciples had seen a similar great haul of fish in Luke 5:4–7. In John 21, we see Jesus lovingly deploy the same fish extravaganza on the day He restores Peter as the fish extravaganza He used to call Peter to follow Him and become a fisher of men in Luke 5.

One of the disciples tells Peter that it's Jesus on the shore. Peter got so flustered that he put on his outer garment and then jumped into the water. And when he arrived on the shore, soaking wet, guess who was fixing breakfast?

Jesus.

When we've messed up, we expect retribution, punishment, or abandonment. But that's not what Jesus does. He extends grace and love with sizzling fish over a fire. And even though Jesus asks Peter and the others to bring some of the fish they had caught, Jesus already had fish prepared for them to eat.

You see, Jesus doesn't need what we bring to the table, but He wants it. He wants us. This Christian journey we're on isn't about need. We were never *needed*.

We are always *wanted*.

God's love for us isn't determined by our actions, pedigrees, performances, or résumés. In His great love, God desires to feed and restore us when we've fallen short and gone backward. He didn't create us because He needed us. He created us because He loves us.

So today, if you're feeling like Peter, don't go fishing. Seek your Savior. You'll discover He's waiting to fix breakfast for you too.

Pause
for Quiet Reflection

Intentionally schedule at least fifteen minutes of quiet time before the Lord with pen and paper in hand. Ask Him to still your busy mind and open your heart. Take your time reflecting on these questions, and then write down your answers.

1. None of us is beyond God's grace and forgiveness. Has there ever been a time when you believe you messed up too bad to receive them? Explain.

_____

_____

2. It is tempting to mentally and/or spiritually "go fishing" when we mess up in order to avoid painful confrontations or consequences. Have you ever decided to go fishing? What were the circumstances? How did God draw you back to Himself?

_____

_____

Apply
It Personally

Now that this lesson has provided some insight from the Word about the lengths Jesus takes to restore our relationship with Him, no matter how far we have drifted away, review what you wrote in the Quiet Reflection section above. Spend the next ten minutes in prayer asking God to reveal areas in your life where you may be tempted to return to what's familiar when the going gets tough. Ask Him to give you the strength to operate in His love for you. Remember, specificity is the key.

God has you in the palm of His hand as you walk through this study individually and together as a group. He promises to bring beauty from ashes, so keep walking.

DAY 5: IT'S NEVER TOO LATE

Therefore, if anyone is in Christ, he is a new creation. The old has passed away; behold, the new has come. (2 Corinthians 5:17)

I wonder if the man on the cross tried to remember how it all started. His life probably began like many other—under a mother's loving gaze. I mean, no child *plans* to become a thief, right? But somehow, it *happened*.

Somewhere between the cradle and the cross, he lost his way. He took things that didn't belong to him. He abandoned the man he could have been for a criminal's life that should never have been. So there he hung.

Glancing over at the One hanging on the cross next to his, I wonder if he recognized Jesus with His wounds and bloody face. Had he heard snippets of Jesus' preaching as he dodged from shadow to shadow?

A crowd gathers at their feet, but not for him. Their deep, sorrowful mourning is reserved for this man hanging next to him. The sign above His head says "King of the Jews."

The people call His name. The thief remembers! This *is* the One people kept talking about. The One who heals, restores, and forgives. Love dangled mere feet from the thief, but he couldn't reach it. He couldn't steal it. He could only stare at it.

It's a good thing Love makes house calls.

Through cracked lips and a parched throat, he pleads, "Jesus, remember me when You come into Your kingdom" (Luke 23:42).

How does Jesus respond in Luke 23:43?

_____

_____

The good news for us in this account is that Jesus demonstrates there is no statute of limitations when it comes to His forgiveness and restoration. Even the vilest criminals will be forgiven and accepted by God if they repent and receive His call to believe by faith.

It is never too late.

God's forgiveness waits for all who seek it, regardless of the transgressions. Write out the following verses that confirm this wonderful truth.

Matthew 6:14–15

Numbers 14:19–20

1 John 1:9

Acts 3:19

Some people confess they are scared that they have sinned too much to receive God's forgiveness. Being scared is a good sign! It's the first sign of repentance that leads to asking for His forgiveness.

I remember when my then-husband first took me to church in October 1990. Although I didn't understand the depth of my sin, I certainly remember feeling as though I wasn't good enough to walk inside the church. After all, in church God could actually *see me,* right?

Fast-forward twenty-five years later, and those feelings have reversed. I know the depth of my sin, so I run to God, knowing His amazing grace and Table of forgiveness await. By the grace of God, I have not lost that sense of wonder at God's unfathomable mercy.

Many years later, I read two verses that perfectly sum up my sense of wonder. Perhaps they will bless you as well.

Write out Micah 7:18–19.

_____

_____

Who is a God like You? Who, indeed.

Sometimes the forgiveness exchange happens at the very end of someone's earthly life—such as the thief on the cross. Atheists who have intentionally shunned God their whole lives can come to faith in the triune God on their deathbeds, repent, and receive His forgiveness and eternal life.

It is never too late.

We read and believe by faith that God removes our sins, but what does He do with them according to the following verses?

Isaiah 1:18

_____

_____

Isaiah 43:25

_____

_____

What a perfect way to wrap up our study! God's forgiveness is never ending as He removes our sins and forgives our iniquities *every single day*.

The person in your life who hurt you needs forgiveness just as much as the person in the mirror. There is no time for *stingy forgiveness* in this world, only God's lavish, scandalous, beautiful forgiveness. *For all.*

Tomorrow is uncertain.

Forgive *today*.

Pause
for Quiet Reflection

Intentionally schedule at least fifteen minutes of quiet time before the Lord with pen and paper in hand. Ask Him to still your busy mind and open your heart. Take your time reflecting on these questions, and then write down your answers.

1. **When have you been struck with a sense of wonder at God's amazing love and forgiveness? What were the circumstances?**

_____

_____

2. **What comfort do you derive from knowing it is *never too late* to receive and offer forgiveness? Does that make you more courageous to interact with a hurting, hurtful world?**

_____

_____

Apply
It Personally

Now that this lesson has provided some insight from the Word about forgiving like our Good Shepherd, review what you wrote in the Quiet Reflection section above. Spend the next ten minutes in prayer asking God to soften your heart toward those who have hurt you so that the forgiveness process can begin, find traction, and succeed. Remember, specificity is the key.

God has you in the palm of His hand as you walk through this study individually and together as a group. He promises to bring beauty from ashes, so keep walking.

Small-Group Connection

As a group, take turns discussing some of the things we learned in the homework in Lesson 8.

1. On Day 1, we looked at how Jesus taught forgiveness, and we learned that His most effective teaching was by modeling forgiveness. Do you believe you model a life of forgiveness to those around you? Why or why not?

2. On Day 3, when the sinful woman approached Jesus in Simon's house, Jesus did not take her to task for her past choices. He forgave her so her future choices would look different. Jesus welcomed outcasts into His life. Do you have outcasts in your life or church? Most simply want to fit in and start over. How could you model forgiveness to make their desire a reality?

3. On Day 4, we see Peter's devastating denial of His Savior. Yet, Jesus welcomes Peter with breakfast, love, and forgiveness. When someone wrongs you, what can you learn from Peter's story about forgiveness?

4. We wrapped up our study on Day 5 by reiterating the fact that it is never too late for Jesus to offer us forgiveness. How does that inspire or challenge you?

Searching the Word Together

Look up and read aloud the following verses. Take turns discussing what strikes you most about each regarding our forgiving God.

Luke 23:34

Matthew 18:21–22

Building Deeper Friendships

Forgiveness is a universal language of love and restoration. Are you holding a grudge in your heart during this season of life? How did Lesson 8 alter how you see forgiveness? If possible, pair up with one person you have yet to pair up with and share what has impacted you most from this study and what has inspired you to change how you treat people who hurt you.

Praying as One

Gather back as a group and pray (either have one person pray or several as they feel led) that God will continue to provide you the courage and strength to receive and extend forgiveness as a way of life. Thank God for gathering your group over the past eight lessons and for their commitment to learn about forgiveness together.

Then in a moment of silence, ask each person to pray silently for the other person who shared their story.

Going the Extra Mile

By God's grace, I pray you have learned much throughout this study regarding forgiveness. I pray God moves in your heart to forgive a sibling who hurt you, a parent who wronged you, a friend who betrayed you, a child who rebelled against you.

Now it's time to close the books and get out in the world to show what forgiveness looks like to people who may have never experienced it.

Volunteer at a shelter. Serve food to the homeless. And all the while, let people know that God is for them and never against them. That forgiveness is always possible when God is placed in the center of the situation.

EPILOGUE

Into the pain our Savior stumbled on Good Friday. His body strained against the wooden beam of our sin splintering His skin.

He shuffled down the Via Dolorosa. The crowd lined the street, taking turns spitting on Him and shouting blasphemies—attacking the very essence of His identity.

Jesus dragged our burden of sin with arms stretched between two peoples with polar-opposite agendas. On one side, the Jewish self-proclaimed defenders of right theology; on the other, government-appointed Roman guards suppressing insurrection at all costs.

The sinless Lamb of God hung between two sin-ridden thieves waiting the death that would relieve excruciating pain. One thief shouted curses; the other sought grace.

The enemy slithered in the shadows believing ultimate victory was finally at hand.

Even though we treated the treasure of God like a traitor, Jesus prayed forgiveness in His final moments, "Father, forgive them, for they know not what they do" (Luke 23:34).

He could have prayed, "Father, forgive them their sins." But He didn't. After all, He routinely forgave others their sins. His words from the cross carried a gentler, all-encompassing grace.

Jesus acknowledged that they were *unknowing*. As though He understood they were doing the best they knew how.

Our Creator hung in painful persecution by the created who *knew not what they did*.

And grace flowed down that tree with His blood.

Jesus could have proven His identity and unleashed the power of hell against the evil hearts of men. Instead, "Father, forgive them."

In that moment, our Savior created a place of U-turns.

His words paved an autobahn of grace, a highway of fresh starts where love collides with pain head on.

Abundant life is found in the about-face space of God's grace.

His sacrifice provided the CPR of hope to abandon life's destructive paths. An exit of fresh starts where we behold His grace. His forgiveness. His face.

Forgiveness was so embedded in the core of Jesus that it was one of the last things He said and did while He hung dying for us.

Jesus forgave even when we didn't repent. Even when we crucified Him. Even when we took His grace for granted.

Those at the foot of the cross tried their best not to stare at the gruesome scene, but death is hard to ignore. They saw His gentle, calloused hands, whose touch had meant so much to so many, now pierced straight through.

Jesus' heart ached with the pain of abandonment. Amidst the stench of sweat and blood, hours passed.

Eventually, so did the Son of Man.

But that's not the end of His story or of ours. Good Friday darkened with death, but Easter Sunday dawned with resurrection! The grave could not hold Him. Death was eternally defeated.

The enemy's head was forever crushed under heaven's stomping victory!

The suffering, death, and resurrection of Jesus provides our chief motivation to forgive others.

Abundant living is found only in forgiving like Jesus did.

Like He still does.

Wounds feel like death.

But forgiveness leads to resurrection.

REFERENCES

Bird, Chad. Blog. "The Myth of Forgiving Yourself." Posted January 8, 2016. http://www.chadbird.com/blog/2016/1/8/the-myth-of-forgivingyourself#.Vpj6XbwTfcc.mailto (accessed January 15, 2016).

Clarke, Benjamin. "The Life of Jesus for Young People." London: Henry Hall, 56, Old Bailey, 1868, p. 44.

Cloud, Henry, and John Townsend. *Boundaries in Marriage*. Grand Rapids: Zondervan Publishing House, 1999.

Dommer, Doug. "Prodigal God: The Older Son." Sermon at Salem Lutheran Church, Tomball, Texas. March 28, 2010. vimeo.com/10563574 (accessed October 8, 2016).

———. "Prodigal God: Forgiveness." Sermon at Salem Lutheran Church, Tomball, Texas. February 28, 2010. vimeo.com/9829744 (accessed October 8, 2016).

———. "Prodigal God: Repentance." Sermon at Salem Lutheran Church, Tomball, Texas. March 14, 2010. vimeo.com/10236708 (accessed October 8, 2016).

Dunk, Paul. Christ Holds Fast Blog. *7 Strikes Is Reasonable.* Posted October 12, 2015. http://www.christholdfast.org/blog/7-strikes-is-reasonable (accessed May 3, 2016).

Easton, M. G. Illustrated Bible Dictionary, third edition. London: Thomas Nelson, 1897.

Gibbs, Jeffrey A. *Matthew 1:1–11:1*. Concordia Commentary. St. Louis: Concordia Publishing House, 2006, p. 345.

Luther, Martin. Luther's Works. Volume 79. St. Louis: Concordia Publishing House, 2016, pages 202–3.

Luther, Martin. *The 95 Theses*. http://www.luther.de/en/95thesen.html (accessed October 26, 2016).

Mattson, Ari. Blog. *What Do We Mean by Forgiveness*? Posted July 10, 2015. http://arimattson.blogspot.de/2015/07/what-do-we-mean-by-forgiveness.html?platform=hootsuite (accessed June 8, 2016).

McCain, Paul, ed. *Concordia: The Lutheran Confessions*, second edition. St. Louis: Concordia Publishing House, 2006, pages 419–20.

Patton, George S. "*Speech to the Third Army*." http://genius.com/
Gen-george-patton-speech-to-the-3rd-army-annotated (accessed
October 3, 2016).

Pyle, Donna. *Your Strong Suit: A Bible Study of Ephesians 6:10–18*. Artesian
Ministries LLC and the Lutheran Women's Missionary League, 2012.

Stuart, Ben. "*Overcome Bitterness.*" Breakaway Ministries. Taught October
4, 2011. http://breakawayministries.org/Resources/talks/Overcome-
Bitterness.

Whale, J. S. *The Protestant Tradition: An Essay and Interpretation*.
Cambridge: Cambridge University Press, 1955, pp. 34–35.

ACKNOWLEDGMENTS

This is the page most people skip.

Except you.

You picked up this book, turned to the acknowledgments, and discovered that I acknowledged everyone else under the sun for their inspiration and writing influence.

Not this time.

We have met, you and I—in the mirror.

You see, unforgiveness and bitterness wear the same mask. The facade that says everything is fine, while we rage hard and cry ugly underneath.

You've been there.

Maybe you are there.

This book acknowledges you because it used to be me.

God desires for you to love wholly, live joyfully, and walk humbly.

Today is a new day because Christ makes you new each day.

Even though we haven't really met, and may never meet, I know that you are weary.

Weary of weeping. Frazzled from fighting. Exhausted from exploding.

Well, no more.

This one's for you.

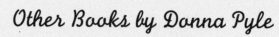

Other Books by Donna Pyle

The God of All Comfort

Quenched

Without This Ring